# Buckle Your Chin Strap

## A Father's Story

Richard J. Williams

*Richard J. Williams*

*To John + his bride,*

*Whenever the trials of life come your way, always remember to*

*"Buckle Your Chin Strap"*

*(RJW)*

D1446119

*www. michaelswings. org*

© 2010 by Richard J. Williams

Published by
Bezalel Books
Waterford, MI
www.BezalelBooks.com

Printed in the United States of America

Cover art by:
Danni Schertzing
Ten4 Design Studio
danni@ten4designstudio.com
www.ten4designstudio.com
c | 517.410.0366

ISBN 978-0-9823388-1-0
Library of Congress Control Number 2009929412

For Amber, Steven and Mollie

How a father, former football player and husband of 26 years copes with and guides his family through his teenage daughter's pregnancy.

# Table of Contents

Chapter 1
Paradise to Reality

Chapter 2
The News – "Sudden Change"

Chapter 3
Decision Time

Chapter 4
The Meeting

Chapter 5
16 and Pregnant – Playing the Game

Chapter 6
Miracle of Life – Inside the Red Zone

Chapter 7
Coming Home – Preparing to Win

Chapter 8
Return to School – You Play Like you Practice

Chapter 9
Summer Vacation? – Will you Sacrifice for the Team?

Chapter 10
Her Senior Year – Play Each Game One Play at a Time

Chapter 11
And Lighting Strikes

Chapter 12
55 Yards to Texas - College and Beyond

Chapter 13
Too Young to Die

# Foreword

This book is being written to help fathers, mothers, pregnant teens, and families cope with the challenges that a teenage pregnancy can bring. When a teenager makes the choice of sex before marriage and becomes pregnant, the consequences are indeed life changing. But they don't necessarily need to be life ending. The life of the unborn child does not need to end. The life and dreams of the teenage mother do not need to end. The life of the grandparents does not end. All roads lead to the same destination. If you are grounded in faith in Christ, you just take the detours. With every decision you make in life, there is a consequence. Consequences occur regardless of the decision you make. The question is what can you live with?

Teenage pregnancy is a tough journey for the entire family. In 2006, our youngest of four children, Mollie, made a choice that will forever change her life and ours. The journey she chose to take was one that gave life to her son Brayden Michael. He was born on April 18, 2007, on his Mom's 17th birthday. What kind of birthday present Brayden was and is shall continue to evolve. As Mollie's parents, the most difficult thing to do was to counsel her on all the decisions and consequences, but to let her make all the decisions. At 16, she surprised us not only with the pregnancy, but with all the decisions she made along the journey.

In writing this book, it is my sincere hope that it can be God's work, not mine. If it helps just one teenager decide to give life to her baby, then God's will be done. If it helps a father guide his family during his teenager's pregnancy, then God's will be done. If it helps the teenager's mother have faith during her daughter's pregnancy experience, then God's will be done. Although it was one of the toughest experiences of my life, it was a blessing. As a football player through high school and college, I learned a valuable lesson. When you get knocked down and you will in life, the most important thing is to get back up and "Buckle Your Chin Strap." Play the next play. In order to play that next play, the Holy Spirit can help you buckle that chin strap if you seek Him and ask Him for His help. He did for me, and my prayer is that He will help you as He did me regardless of your situation in life. May God bless your journey. Buckle your chin strap with the Lord and He will help you all win in any worthy endeavor you are fighting for in the end.

# CHAPTER ONE
## Paradise to Reality

*Matthew Chapter 7 Verses 24 and 25*
*"Everyone who listens to those words of mine and acts*
*on them will be like a wise man who built his house on*
*rock. The rain fell, the floods came and the winds blew*
*and buffeted the house but it did not collapse; it had*
*been set solidly on rock"*

There are many times in your life that you will journey from paradise back to reality. As quickly as we get our glimpses of paradise, suddenly we can be shocked back to reality. It is important that we build our house on the rock of faith in Jesus Christ. Many times on my life's journey I have cruised between paradise and back to reality. I have been blessed to have built my house on the rock of Christ Jesus to withstand the storms and winds of challenge. A teenage pregnancy is an example of the wind buffeting your house. Will you let those winds cause your house to collapse or will you buckle your chin strap and play the next play?

How many times in your life have you journeyed to paradise and been shocked back to reality? In 1975, after graduating from Lumen Christi High School, a Catholic high school in the small rural town of Jackson, Michigan, I learned this for the first time. In high school, I was captain of the football team, all-area, all-state and never came off the field from the opening kickoff until the final second ticked away in our weekly football games. I played guard on offense, linebacker on defense and every special teams play in every game. I was in paradise and did not realize it, until going away to college that first fall in 1975. Upon my arrival to Grand Valley State University, a small NCAA Division II school, I quickly learned this lesson. I was no longer the big fish in a small pond. I was a little tiny guppy in Lake Michigan and was shocked to learn that I really would have to work hard to compete at this level. I went from paradise to reality real quick. The players on the team were bigger, faster and stronger than me and I had my hands full if I was going to make the travel team, much less be a starter.

The very first day on my arrival to Grand Valley State, I almost left before I got started. My father drove me to camp late July on a hot and muggy Saturday morning for my first college football camp experience. It was about a two hour drive that seemed to take an eternity. I was very nervous and anxious to arrive and did not talk much with my Dad during the ride there. I think he shared in my anxiety as the two of us drove stoically to Allendale, Michigan, which is a rural town ten miles west of Grand Rapids, Michigan.

We pulled into the College Landing and drove the slow and winding curves into the campus and searched for the Football Team's Check-In Headquarters. When we finally found the Kistler dormitory where camp check-in was, my Dad who is still the toughest and smartest man I ever knew, got out of the car and handed me my suitcase. I did not know whether I should hug him or cry as the man who introduced me to the game I loved, now prepared to say goodbye to his oldest son. He quickly extended his hand and shook it in his vice grip and said "Goodbye and Good Luck." My father worked very hard growing up in the depression and worked in a drop forge factory his entire life along with many other odd jobs to support our family of six children. He is about six feet tall and weighs 280 pounds with a burly chest and Popeye forearms, and ran the largest hammer press that literally pounded billets of hot molten steel into truck hubs and large car axles. The hubs usually weighed in excess of one hundred pounds so you can imagine how physically strong and tough my father was back in his day. My friends were scared to death of him and never wanted to shake his hand for fear that he would break it as he had very strong hands from handling the molten steel with 30 pound steel tongs eight hours a day, six days a week. It was very difficult to say this goodbye to him. As I turned to enter the dorm, I had a huge lump in my throat, but managed to swallow real hard when I was greeted by my first teammate who stood immediately before me. My first teammate that I met was Daryl Gooden, who was a junior, an African American from Romulus High School in Romulus, Michigan. Daryl stood about 6' 1" and weighed 260 pounds with an afro that made him appear four inches taller or about six foot five. He had not an ounce of fat on his body and was ripped with solid muscles popping out all over the place. He was wearing a sleeveless tee shirt which my brothers and I knew simply as a "Grandpa Williams" tee shirt.

Some people today refer to them as wife beaters but I prefer to call them simply "Grandpa Williams" shirts in memory of my grandpa who lived right next door to me when I grew up. He always wore these tee shirts despite not having the muscles normally associated with this style. Daryl had a 20-inch neck and trapezoid muscles that went from his ear lobe to his shoulder and huge pectoral and bicep/tricep muscles. Around his neck he wore a 1 inch choker chain normally reserved for large dogs like Great Danes, Saint Bernard's or Tigers, Lions, etc. with the letters "S.O.L.D."

I had no idea what the letters stood for and there was no way I was going to ask him. Heck, I wanted to stay alive. When he shook my hand and introduced himself, I felt like the smallest guy on earth. I turned to look at my Dad who was pulling away in his 1974 white Pontiac Lemans, and I swear to God, I wanted to run to the car, jump in and go back home! What was I getting myself into? I knew that my Dad and my high school coaches would be disappointed if I whimped out. But was I big and tough enough to knock heads with the likes of Daryl Gooden and stay connected to my anatomy? I decided I better just try to "buckle my chin strap" and by the grace of God I endured that first two weeks of college football camp my freshman year.

That was probably to that point, my biggest test in life. More tests were to come, that much was certain. As for Daryl, he turned out to be one of the greatest men I ever played with. After graduating, he worked as a social worker helping the poor and destitute in Detroit until he died my senior year two years after his graduation. He died helping a stranded motorist change her flat tire on the side of a busy highway in Metropolitan Detroit. A car had lost control suddenly and side swiped him while he was removing her flat tire. He died on the scene from multiple bone fractures and head trauma. What a way to end your life and greet your maker. He was helping this lady whom he did not know, just like he tried to help me and make me feel welcome that first day of college football camp. He was a good teammate and great person. He shocked me to reality on my arrival from high school to college. He also shocked me in the reality that life is a gift each day we live in the tragic, but sacrificial way he died. He was my first experience of death to someone my age or younger, but unfortunately not the last.

In another paradise to reality experience in my first college football camp at Grand Valley State, I got in my first and only football fight. During football camp we practiced three times a day. We would rise at

6:00am, eat breakfast at 6:30am and practice in shorts and helmets for 90 minutes from 7:30am until 9:00am. After that first practice we would meet with position coaches from 9:30am until 10:30am reviewing film, techniques or schemes. At 11:30am, we would have lunch and then be out in full pads by 12:30 p.m. until 2 p.m. Then we would get an hour break and at 3:30 p.m. until 5:30 p.m. we would practice again in full pads. After this third practice was finished, we would have dinner and be in a 7:00 p.m. meeting with the entire team. In these nightly meetings, we would hear philosophy talks on life, team and football from our head coach Jim Harkema, or occasionally watch a movie. By 10:00 p.m. we had to be in bed for room check and then try to sleep in a hot, small dorm room with 2 bunk beds and no ventilation. We called the rooms "sauna closets" as they were hot and about as small as a walk-in closet with two bunk beds. Needless to say, after a day in football camp, you were exhausted.

In any event, my first football fight occurred on probably the 9th or 10th day of my freshman camp. We had a drill called front seven. It was a drill whereby the front seven offensive linemen would run block for a running back who tried to run the ball through seven defensive linemen. It was a late afternoon 3:30 p.m. practice. It was a very hot and muggy 90° day and by this point of camp many players had either quit, went home, gotten injured or the ones left were tired, ornery and short on patience. It was my turn to be on the offensive line and I lined up for the play. We ran the play, and there was a linebacker, who was named Danny Jackson that I was up against. I was an offensive tackle that first year and lined up at left offensive tackle in this particular drill. Danny had forearms that were akin to Mohammed Ali jabs. He could literally knock you down with a quick forearm to the head. I went low to cut Danny off and kept driving him and then the whistle blew. After the whistle blew, Danny hauled off with one of his patented inside forearm shots to the side of my head and knocked me down face first to the ground. I don't know if it was the heat, the exhaustion or both, but I jumped up off the ground and started pummeling him with swings to the head. I had never done this before or after, but I came unglued. I went absolutely crazy. Luckily for me, the defensive coordinator Coach Bill Hardy, an African American, who had played defensive tackle for the University of Michigan, jumped in and pulled me away and said, "Good job Dick Williams, don't take any of that stuff from him. Now go back to the huddle." I retreated back to the offensive side where I was promptly greeted by my offensive line coach Bruce Zylstra who became a good friend of mine. Bruce was in his first year of college coaching. Prior to coming to Grand Valley State, Bruce or "Coach Z" as we called him, was the Head Football Coach for Hudsonville High School, a local West Michigan Public School. Coach Z told me to get a drink and take a break. Little did I know who Danny Jackson was at the time. He was a junior All American linebacker who led the team in tackles. After getting a drink, I came back to the drill.

When I got back to the drill, the only senior offensive lineman on our team Danny Karpowicz pulled me aside and said, "Hey rookie are you crazy? Do you know who you just got into a fight with?" I said "No, who is he?" He said, "That is "Danny Jackson" from Detroit Martin Luther King High School and he is the toughest "blankety blank" on this team." It seems in my frustration, I had retaliated in a fight with the guy most respected and feared on the team. After this episode, I won the respect of the team and admiration of the coaching staff, but never fought in a football uniform again. I did end up making the travel team my freshman year as a second string offensive left tackle. I played on punts and kickoff return specialty teams earning a varsity letter as a true freshman. By my sophomore year, I was a starter and started my remaining three years as an offensive guard. I was blessed to receive a college degree through football. But the greatest education I received were the lessons I learned on the gridiron. For those I would be eternally grateful to my high school football coach Jim Crowley.

Jim Crowley is a legend in the town of Jackson, Michigan. He started Lumen Christi's football program in 1969 which has won several state championships. Lumen Christi is the Latin word for the "Light of Christ." Mr. Crowley was about as close to the Latin Word for Light of Christ that you could get. He truly was God's Light. He was the strict disciplinarian and most of his players feared him. Many would quit as was the case my senior year in high school due to their fear or lack of will to endure the work and sacrifice necessary to accomplish his goals, which quickly became your goals.

In the spring before my senior and final high school year, at least a dozen or more of my classmates had quit, forgoing their senior year. Many of them had much more talent than me, or other guys left on the team. We ended up with only six seniors returning that next fall and only two of us were starters. I will never forget what Coach Crowley did that spring afternoon in 1974. I was in Mr. Arpino's class that day. Mr. Arpino taught government and political science classes and was a great teacher/coach in his own right, and led our cross country and track teams to many state championships as well. Suddenly, I was called to Mr. Crowley's office through the intercom system in Mr. Arpino's room. Coach Crowley was also the assistant principal and was the disciplinarian for the school. If you were called to his office from a teacher's room on the intercom, it usually meant you were in some kind of trouble. Most likely you were in big trouble. As I walked the long walk to his office, a thousand questions ran through my mind. "What did I do wrong?" Was I at a party this past weekend with drinking going on?" Did I miss an assignment or do poorly on a recent test?" Did I offend a teacher? When I finally arrived at his office, he was smoking a big stogie, which he usually reserved for momentous occasions. Like after a win over a tough opponent. He told me to sit down. I did as he instructed and he began "The Speech." He started out, "Dick, do you know what a leader is?" I swallowed hard and thought oh no, I must have done something that was not leader oriented. The smoke from his Cuban cigar was circling around my neck and seemed to be choking me for the right answer. I said reluctantly, "Yes Coach." He went on to say that a leader of his football teams was a guy he could count on always to do the right thing. Leaders are always first in every drill line. In every sprint or agility exercise, leaders are first. Leaders work harder than anyone else on the team. They set the bar for the rest of the team through example. Leaders take the fall for their teammates. Leaders are willing to sacrifice for the good of the team. He asked me, "Dick, do you want to be a leader of this team next year?" I said, "Yes, coach, if you want me to be, I will try my best."

I was somewhat relieved by now, knowing that I was not in any kind of trouble. But I was still sitting erect and on the edge of my seat. He went on to say, "The first thing I need you to do then, is switch positions." I thought wow, what was that going to mean? Maybe I could switch back to running back. My first two years of high school, I played the running back position on offense, and then they switched me to tight end/wide receiver my junior year. I played linebacker on defense all four years. I was anxious to hear that I was going to be switched back to running back, since I knew of course I was a "skilled position" player. To my dismay, coach announced, "I need you to switch to offensive guard" on offense. He looked at my face to study my reaction. I had never played on the offensive line ever. How could he want me, a guy who had played quarterback and running back all my life to switch to the offensive line? "Is he crazy or what?" I thought. Luckily, I remained calm and somehow answered immediately the answer he was searching for. I said, "Coach, if that will help our team and help me be the leader you want, I will do whatever you ask." In the four years from ninth grade in high school to my freshman year in college, I grew 15 inches and put on 110 pounds. I was still growing that spring 1974 of my junior year, and thanks to Coach Crowley, he made my most important position switch in all my years of football. He could see that I was still growing. He could also see that my best chance of playing in college and obtaining a scholarship was either as a guard or linebacker. He knew that our team also needed help on the offensive line and he asked me to sacrifice and do what was best for our team.

Little did I know, during "The Speech," that he was hand picking me to be the leader of the team that would start only two seniors, five sophomores and eleven juniors the fall of 1974. I was one of three of us that played both ways, on offense and defense. Coach Crowley also told me in the speech that he was going to send me to a leadership camp at Central Michigan University that summer sponsored by fellowship of Christian Athletes. I would not have to pay for the camp as it was being donated by a donor. I was thrilled to attend the camp and learned a lot of things about leadership on and off the playing field from a Christian athlete's perspective.

As my reward for being the leader that 1974 autumn of his team, Coach Crowley put me up for all types of recognition awards, made a highlight film of my good plays and personally called college coaches he knew. He sent copies of the highlight film to them for review. Back then in 1974, this was virtually unheard of making highlight films of high school players for college coaches to review. He was a pioneer back in the day in how to obtain scholarships for his players.

I often think of Coach Crowley who died far too young at the age of 46 from a gunshot wound to his neck in an armed robbery incident. After picking up his seven year old daughter from the ice skating rink he was robbed at gunpoint. A struggle occurred and the bullet went through his neck killing him in his backyard. The man who shot him was captured years later, but had just gotten out of prison that day. Jackson is a town known for having Michigan's largest prison. The perpetrator was looking for a quick heist on his way back to Detroit with his cousin to get some money. He had cased the party store for a few minutes and saw my coach come in with a wad of money. My coach also sold real estate on the side and had just cashed a large commission check earlier that day. So when he entered the store to buy a gallon of milk he pulled out his "coach" money clip and showcased the large sum of money he had on him.

The perpetrators saw the money and followed him to his home, most likely figuring it would be an easier hit than the party store. The murderers jumped him in his driveway in front of his daughter whom he told to run into the house. They shot him in the neck and fled back to Detroit. Coach Crowley bled to death in his own backyard, a brutal and senseless way to die. This was my second shock from paradise back to reality in how precious the gift of life is. I would not have been prepared for many of the things that have happened in my life, much less "The News" in 2006 had Mr. Crowley not given me the speech and the opportunity to play college football. "The Speech" will forever be tattooed in my heart and I have played it back thousands of times over the years to help me "buckle my chin strap" and keep playing the game of life.

In July of 2006, I experienced God's natural paradise in the Hawaiian Islands. My wife and soulmate Linda, whom I had been married to for 25 years, went there for two weeks to celebrate our 25th wedding anniversary. We had been planning and saving for the trip for 3 ½ years. When we were married at age 24, we could not afford an elaborate honeymoon since we had paid for much of our wedding and the associated expenses ourselves. We went to Traverse City, Michigan, a small resort town on Lake Michigan, in the northwestern region of Michigan for just a few days. We enjoyed a few days up there after our wedding and came home to get back to work. That was our first honeymoon and to us it was great, but it was not the paradise that Hawaii is.

As we approached our first milestone anniversary number 25, we thought, let's take a second honeymoon this time to the Hawaiian Islands. We planned or should I say, Linda planned the entire trip. From Pearl Harbor to Waikiki Beach to our first and last helicopter ride, and to the Road to Hana. She planned it all. For three and a half years we saved every extra cent we could manage between paying for two kids' college tuition, car payments, mortgage, insurance and every day bills. Thank God for Linda. She is the planner in our house. She had every detail thought out and even had contingency plans in case the weather did not allow us to do the planned activities. We golfed three of Hawaii's most difficult and pristine golf courses. We snorkeled off the shoreline of Maui. We ate at wonderful restaurants like Mama's Fish House, Sorrento's, Dukes, Fred's and Capiche. We relaxed on the beaches of Lahani and Kapalua. It was the most beautiful place I have ever visited in my life. Linda and I felt as if we were in paradise and neither one of us wanted to return home.

We were blessed to travel with two of our dearest friends the Strock's, Don and Judy, who also celebrated their 25th wedding anniversary on this trip. Don and I planned a special ceremony on the beach where we renewed our wedding vows with our brides as the sun set on the beaches of Walileia in Maui, Hawaii. It was the one and only thing we had planned to surprise our brides. We enjoyed champagne as the tropical red sun set and even nicknamed the point the Strock/Williams peninsula.

This vacation in Hawaii to celebrate 25 years of marriage truly was God's glimpse of natural paradise, but too soon it was back to reality in Canton, Michigan, where neither of us knew the shock we were about to receive upon our arrival home.

*Luke Chapter 24 Verse 43*
*"Amen I say to you, today you will be with me in paradise."*

 As Jesus struggles in a myriad of pain on the cross to breathe His last breaths, His persecutors and tormentors were still present in the others crucified with Him. Those with little faith implored Him to save Himself and come down from that cross and save them too. There was one next to him that scolded the others for their lack of faith and asked Jesus to remember him when He comes into His kingdom. Jesus told him, "Amen I say to you, today you will be with me in paradise."

While we journey here on earth in our realities of life, will we be the tormentor and persecutors of Jesus when challenges come? Or will we be like the man who was crucified with Jesus who admitted that he was a sinner and asked to be remembered in His kingdom? Will we be unified with Christ in our suffering or will we be like those who questioned and taunted the Lord?

Jesus assured us all through his final breath that we can be in paradise if we simply accept our realties of life and be crucified with Him in faith. Buckle Your Chin Strap with faith and you can journey to paradise from your earthly reality.

# Chapter 2
# The News

*Luke Chapter 10 Verse 21*
*"I give you praise, Father, Lord of heaven and earth, for*
*although you have hidden these things from the wise*
*and learned, you have revealed them to the childlike."*

Many times in life, things of major importance can be right in front of you but hidden. In our case, our teenage daughter was pregnant due to an unfortunate choice she made to have premarital sex. But there was a life, a soul growing, hidden inside her womb. If you were to ask a young child, "Do you think we should kill the baby growing inside because the mother is only 16?" The child would most certainly exclaim, "No way!" The baby has a right to live. God's will for each of us is to enjoy the lovemaking act with our married husband/wife joined in His sacrament of marriage. However, He reveals to His children that even unwed teenage pregnant girls should give their babies life. Thankfully, He revealed that to our Mollie and to us as His children. Be like a child when it comes to making choices in your life and God will reveal His ways.

After spending almost a day in four crowded airports between all the stops from Maui, to Honolulu, to Los Angeles, to Detroit, we finally arrived home at about six o'clock in the morning. Linda and I were both exhausted as neither of us could sleep on the airplane. As I unloaded the suitcases, Linda decided to get the mail. Our next door neighbor had been collecting our mail while we were gone, but there were still a few items in the mailbox from the day before. One of the envelopes was an unstamped letter addressed to my wife. As she opened it, she remarked, "this is weird, I wonder who this is from?" As she read the letter, I watched her look go from bewilderment to horror in an instant. The letter said:

> Dear Linda,
> You do not know me. I have tried over the past couple weeks to reach you by telephone discreetly, but have been unsuccessful. A couple weeks ago while my daughter and her friends were in our basement, I overheard them talking about Mollie Williams who thought she was pregnant. My daughter thought I was away shopping and did not know I had overheard their conversation. After her girlfriends went home, I confronted her about spreading vicious rumors like these and how it can damage or ruin a girl's reputation. She assured me though that it was not a rumor, but that it was true. I just thought you and your family should know so you can deal with the situation as you see fit.

The letter was unsigned.

Linda handed me the letter and I read it. My heart went numb, while my mind raced with questions and thoughts. This can't be true. Not our Mollie. She has never even had a boyfriend. Maybe it was a different Mollie, a case of mistaken identity. Who could the father be? Why wouldn't she tell us? Why did she do this? Was it a rape? This was not the news I wanted nor did I suspect was even remotely true. Our Mollie was the kindest and meekest soul of all of our children. There is no way that God would let this happen to her.

As you can imagine, going on no sleep for over 24 hours, our bodies received an instant shot of adrenalin. We initially cried together, but decided not to waste anymore emotion on it until we talked with Mollie. Although it was 6:30am now in the morning, we needed to wake Mollie up and talk with her. She had stayed with her best friend Samantha while we were gone.

Samantha and Mollie met in the second grade and have been best friends ever since. We did not want to call on a Sunday morning at 6:30am, but we had to get to the bottom of this.

Linda made the call. "Robin?" "Yeah," she said. "This is Linda, I am very sorry to call you so early in the morning. Dick and I are home, but we need Mollie to wake up as we have an urgent family situation that we need to talk with her about." " I'll go get her," Robin said. "Oh no," Linda exclaimed, "We are coming over there to pick her up right now. Have her gather her things and be ready." On the way over to Samantha's house, Linda and I did not speak a word. It was the longest five minute ride of my life. We were both in shock and we both feared the worst had arrived. Neither of us knew what to do, what to say or how to handle this situation. Thankfully, our help came from the Lord.

When Mollie came out of Samantha's house, she had an inquisitive look on her tired face, but she seemed quite happy to see us. "Hi Mom, hi Dad, what's wrong?" she said. I told her that we were going to wait until we got home to discuss the matter and tried to small talk on the way back. After all, with a high school of over 6000 kids, chances are there was another Mollie Williams there that was pregnant. Not my Mollie. I was not going to push the panic button just yet.
As we pulled into our driveway, the sun was just sparkling over the rustling, fully-leafed trees from a

soft summer breeze in our backyard. It seemed to be saying, "Don't worry Dad, everything will be all right."

We went into the house. We told Mollie to go sit down in the den. That is when she knew it was serious. Over the years, whenever we had a serious family matter to discuss, we always did so in the den. Our den is a very small room, but cozy. It has a small two seat couch, a chair and a little 19-inch television on a rectangular shaped oak stand and a small round oak table next to the couch. The room is decorated in a golf theme with pictures of my favorite golfers and all sorts of golf memorabilia. There was no place to run when we shut the door to the den. It was as if you were in a mother's womb, warm, close and a place of love. Mollie sat down and we began the talk. Linda said, "We have been up for over 24 hours in airports coming home and when we came home, I found this letter in the mailbox. "I want you to read it," she exclaimed. As Linda handed her the letter, I was still sure that Mollie would read it and start laughing, as surely it was another Mollie Williams. Not my Mollie Williams. As I studied her face while she read the letter, I realized in an instant that I was wrong. Dead wrong! Mollie's facial expression turned suddenly pale and her eyes started to tear up. I thought, "No Lord Jesus! How could this be happening? Why Lord? Why are you persecuting us with this? Her life is going to be ruined and what are we going to do? How can I fix this? Lord, please wake me up from this terrible nightmare! This cannot be happening to Mollie! Why Lord? What are we going to do? How could You let this happen, Lord? I have tried to be your faithful servant! Why Lord?"

The next few moments were spent firing questions at her in rapid fire. First by Linda, and then by me. Is this true? When did it happen? Where did it happen? Who was the boy? Did he wear a condom? Was it done in his house or our house? Were his parents home? Did he force himself on you? Did you tell him he could enter you? Why did you put yourself in this situation? Don't we always have a rule that the parents must be home if you go to a friend's house? Where were Mom and I? How long has it been since your last period? When did it happen? Was it rape? On and on the questions went like this for well over a half hour.

Finally, I looked at Linda and said, "Well, we need to find out if her suspicion is true, Mollie have you taken a pregnancy test?" Mollie was only 16 years old and had only been having her menstrual period for a year or so. She did not even know about what or how a home pregnancy test was performed. She thought you needed to go to the doctor to perform a blood test. I told her to sit tight; Dad was going to fix this. I jumped into my car and drove to the local supermarket to look for a pregnancy test kit. As I drove the car, I prayed, "Dearest Lord Jesus, please let this pregnancy test be negative. Lord I beg of you, please Lord, don't let this be happening to my precious darling little girl." I could not get to the store quick enough. It was almost a seven minute drive to the store, since I had to go to a super store that was open 24 hours. As I entered the store, I suddenly realized, "How will I know which section of the super store a pregnancy test would be located?" I wondered out loud, "Where would a pregnancy test kit be found?" I knew it would most likely be found in the pharmacy. But what were people going to think when a guy my age, "49" asked for a pregnancy test kit? Isn't that something that the woman usually buys? Sure enough, as you probably can guess, I could not find the pregnancy test kits. I looked all over with no luck. I had to ask the pharmacy technician, who was a very intelligent looking young Asian lady. "Excuse me miss, can you help me find one of those home pregnancy test kits?" She looked at me for a moment awkwardly, and said, "Sure they are back here behind the medicine rack." "What kind would you like?" she asked. I thought for a moment, "Why is she asking me that?" "I want the one that will work, I thought, but one that will show a negative pregnancy result." So I remarked, "I don't know, my wife usually buys these, just give me the one that is the most accurate." She laid three of them on the counter for me to choose. I was not in the mood to ask further questions and wanted out of there so fast, I just grabbed the first one. Feeling embarrassed, I paid for the kit as quickly as possible and sped home. As I traveled home, it occurred to me, "Why didn't you buy two of them? What if the first one gets contaminated in the test and turns out positive? Shouldn't you get another one? Turn back you dummy, and go and get another one." By now I was running short on patience and energy. I decided to continue my ride home and just do the test.

When I arrived home, Linda and Mollie were still sitting in the den. Both of them looked scared and borderline terrified. Being the big tough guy and former football player, I was sure I could settle them down and fix this tense situation. I got the pregnancy kit out of the bag and started reading the directions. Linda was so nervous and exhausted she sat on the couch almost listless as I told Mollie what to do. "Just go urinate in a cup and then I will pour your urine on this sampling stick, in order to administer the test. After I do that, we have to wait a couple minutes for the results." Mollie headed to the bathroom and nervously delivered me her sample of urine. I took out the directions again and read them to make certain I would apply the test in the correct manner. Once I poured the urine on the sampling stick, I set it upright as the box described. We left the stick on the counter and started praying once again. Please Lord; please don't let Mollie be pregnant. Please let the result be negative. Please don't let the line show up. We all held hands and prayed together in silence. Mollie and Linda were so frightened I could feel both of them shaking and trembling from the fear.

After a couple of minutes, I crept to the bathroom counter like a snake ready to pounce on an unsuspecting prey and found the result. The line was barely visible but enough of a line appeared to show the result was positive. I showed it to Mollie and Linda, and the screams shrieked throughout our entire house. I had only heard my wife cry like that once before in my life, but that is a different story and another time. Mollie and Linda were bawling, sobbing and shrieking screams of sorrow unlike any I have ever heard, or wanted to hear again. This was something I had to fix. "This test might be wrong," I said, "Look the line is very shaded and is not dark and continuous like the directions show. Maybe this test is inaccurate or contaminated. Let me go back to the store and get another one."

This time my journey back to the supermarket was truly one that seemed like I was on a treadmill going no where fast. How could this be happening? "This test must be wrong, I kept saying to myself. I have to fix this. Lord Jesus, please fix this for me. I don't know what to do." When I finally got to the store, I literally ran from the parking lot into the store to the pharmacy section and located a different pharmacy clerk. This time I did not care the least what she thought, I just needed another pregnancy test and to get back home, so I could fix this situation once and for all. "Give me two of these please," as I showed her the box from the first pregnancy test kit I had bought. Luckily, I had remembered to bring the empty box with me. This time I made certain to get an extra one so we could try a third time if necessary. She gave me the two HPT kits and I raced home. In the back of my mind, maybe it was Satan, I don't know, but I swear I heard the tune from the Wizard of Oz when the wicked witch is riding her bike. I could not shut it off. I could not believe the nightmare that had become my reality. Only a short while ago, I was in paradise in Hawaii. Now I was in a reality that was almost surreal. I could not get home fast enough.

When I finally got home the second time, Linda was a wreck and Mollie, bless here tender heart was rolled up into a ball trembling on the couch in the den. I told her, reassuringly, "Mollie, there is a significant chance that the first test was wrong." I continued my appeal to her in a comforting tone, "This time rather than peeing in a cup, just hold the sampling stick and submerge it over the urine stream so that the filter section can absorb the urine." This is what the directions had said to do the first time, but I figured the cup technique would work, and that way Linda could just relax as she was exhausted. I knew I had to fix this.

So Mollie reluctantly re-entered the bathroom and performed a second home pregnancy test. This time the result was undeniably positive. The line was dark and vibrant blue. I wanted to vomit, I felt sick to my stomach. Poor Mollie, she did not deserve this. We did not deserve this. What were we going to do? It seemed the big tough football player couldn't fix this after all!

Perplexed, I decided to encourage Mollie to wait an hour and then we would do a third test, with the extra HPT kit I had purchased just to make sure. I immediately got her a glass of orange juice and told her to drink it. An hour went by and we administered the third and final home pregnancy test. Strike three batters out! Positive! Mollie was pregnant at 16. What were we going to do?

Linda and I discussed it and decided, let's go to the doctor's office and do the blood work test first to be

100% sure. She called our doctor and explained the situation to the nurse. Although they were booked with appointments, the nurse was kind enough to tell us to come right up and they would work us in. On our drive to the doctor's office, not a word was spoken. As we drove there, it was as if the world had ended and we were on our way to greet the Lord. None of us wanted to be in the car, much less traveling to a doctor to confirm the news that none of us wanted confirmed. It was surreal.

When we checked into the reception area, I could not help but notice a new mother with her newborn infant son waiting to be seen. She had a look of joy that only a parent has when their new bundle arrives. It was as if it were a sign that everything would be O.K. As we went over to find a seat in the reception area, I saw an elderly man with a patch over his right eye and a cane on his lap and another mom with two of her three kids wrestling while the sick one was listlessly lying in her arms. I could not help, but think, "Lord this is still my nightmare, right? I am dreaming all this. Wake me up from my nightmare Lord, I've had enough."

"Mollie Williams," the nurse called suddenly from the doorway. We all jumped up. No, it was not a dream. This was happening and we would soon be in the doctor's office drawing blood. We were promptly escorted to an examination room.

Once in the cold and plainly decorated exam room, we had to explain again why we were there. "Mollie may be pregnant," Linda said. We want to get a lab test and blood work to confirm it. "When was your last period?" asked the nurse. Mollie said she was not sure, but about two and a half months earlier. We told her about the three home pregnancy tests that we administered and the positive results of each. She drew the blood and urine for the tests and then we sat and waited once again. There is something about waiting for news that you don't want to hear, that makes time stand still. You are almost frozen in time as your mind wanders and you try to think of something other than what ails you. After what seemed like two hours, but was most likely only 30 minutes, there was a knock at the door and the doctor scurried her way in. She was a pediatrician and I do not believe she was comfortable in telling us the "The News." She tried to small talk for the first couple minutes of our awkward introduction and then abruptly asked, "Well do you want to know the results?" If looks could kill, I think that doctor would have been drilled. I wanted to throw a forearm shiver to her head, and say no, we have only been waiting here for hours so you could put us through this torment. "Did you ever hear of grace, humility and kindness, much less bedside manners?" I thought. It was with all the grace I could muster, to first reply a simple but firm, "Yes." This doctor had little if any tact and it was almost as if she was relishing playing with our emotions in giving us the news. "Yes, it's positive, she is pregnant." You will need to see an OBGYN and get her vitamins. She mumbled something about "Planned Parenthood" which went right by me at the time. However, afterward it hit me; she was insinuating that we get her an ABORTION!

Lord how can this be happening to us? Our poor Mollie and her life are ruined. But thankfully I heard this little voice inside me say "Dick, it will be all right first Buckle Your Chin Strap and play the next play." I believe that voice was the Holy Spirit.

In the next few days we hunkered down in our home. I called in sick to work and the three of us just literally sat limp in our house. One of Mollie's other close friends who already knew of her possible pregnancy, came over and spent the next four nights at our house comforting, consoling and just "being there" for Mollie. Thank the good Lord for Morgan. Mollie really needed someone other than her shocked parents to reassure her that everything was going to be all right. Her brothers and sister were away or at college and there was no one who could comfort her more than a friend like Morgan.

Looking back now, I can see that the signs were there. I had coached Mollie in soccer from age five through fourteen and I knew her like a book. A few weeks before we left for our 25th anniversary and second honeymoon to Hawaii, I had noticed that she was quiet and seemed sad. I had in fact asked her several times "What's the matter Mollsles?" which was my nickname for her. She would reply the usual remark, "Nothing Dad". But I knew in my heart something was wrong. On the second day of our hunkering down in our home, with Morgan there I asked her. "Mollie, is that why you were so quiet before we went to Hawaii?" When I kept asking you what was wrong, I knew that something was bothering you." She said, "Yeah Dad. I was scared and I was ashamed." What a burden she had carried around with her. The weight of the world was upon her shoulders. She did not want to disappoint me or Linda, and she did not know where to turn. Obviously, the rumor mill at school had caught up with the anonymous note lady, which we thankfully had received in our mailbox. I would like to believe that Mollie would have eventually told us, but the damage it would have done to her conscious, her self esteem and her soul could have ruined her. We were thankful that whoever put that note in our mailbox did so.

I have always tried my best to be a good father for my children. I am by no means perfect and have many faults. I remember when Mollie played soccer for me. She would cry if the ball hit her in the stomach or got kicked in the shin. How in the world was she going to deliver a baby? Should she deliver the baby? What is going to happen? Many questions and things go through your mind. In retrospect, it was a good thing to do, take our time to get over the initial shock and just "hunker down." It gave us all time to cry, laugh, analyze and pray.

When your teenage daughter gets pregnant, it is something that society says you should be ashamed of. These things were better off kept hush, hush and in fact talked of very little out in the open. My instincts told me to talk with people I could trust and ones who were either in positions that have encountered this before, or experienced this themselves.

I first decided to speak with my friend Joe who was a retired Chief of Police. I did not know what the law was regarding sex with a minor. I still believed in my heart that this boy had forced himself on my daughter even though Mollie had consistently told me that it was consensual. Joe told me to file a police report. He said it was a "statutory rape" even if it was consensual sex. He was a good friend and a Christian brother whom I could trust. He also advised me to call a lawyer.

After speaking to a lawyer on two, 5-minute phone calls, where I did most of the talking, I received a $200 bill. I was told I could do nothing legally until the paternity of the child was determined after the baby was born. He also said I could file a police report if I wanted. I was very disappointed in the advice I received and realized for the first time in my life that you should always try to avoid legal matters as they can be very expensive.

The next person I reached out to was my cousin Debbie. Debbie turned out to give me the best advice of anyone. Debbie was three years older than me, and we grew up across the street from each other on Hamilton Street. Hamilton Street was a dead-end street that ran two city blocks long near the old stone walled state penitentiary. The folks on Hamilton Street were all lower middle class people who loved their children and their faith. Most of us were either relatives or Catholics who attended St. John's Catholic elementary school and church. She was the queen of "Hamilton Street" and to most of us also the King. Until our teenage years, she was the toughest boy/girl in the land. At 17, Debbie also got pregnant. Thankfully, for Mollie it was a different time and era. To my dismay, I listened as Debbie recalled and told me of her nightmare that occurred some 40 years earlier and was one of the cruelest stories I have ever heard.

She was so afraid to tell her parents in the early 1970s that she was pregnant, she just hid it by wearing baggy clothes. Finally, as she neared being six months along, she told her mom, who told her dad (my aunt and uncle). Uncle Jim was a large man well over 300 pounds about six feet and everyone in the whole neighborhood including his nephew was frightened of him. He had a deep manly voice that was gruff. I would have been terrified to tell him as well. His own children nicknamed him "Large" and Aunt Barb was known simply as "Bubbles." In any event, as you can imagine they were very upset about Debbie's pregnancy. The doctors told them they should get Debbie an abortion even though she was six months pregnant, catholic and knowledgeable that abortion is killing an innocent human being. She was a year older than Mollie as she was 17, and already in her senior year of high school. "Large" however, put a stop to their doctor's advice that had her on the next train to a New York City chop shop that was to do the abortion. He would not let them take her to NY to have the "procedure" done. They knew it was too late in the pregnancy to do an abortion and Debbie would be in jeopardy of losing her life if she went there and had the "procedure" done.

Uncle Jim finally relented and let Debbie stay home to have the baby on three conditions. First, she had to go away and have it. He did not want shame on his family. Second, she had to give it up for adoption. No way was a bastard going to live with them. Lastly, she was not allowed to speak of her baby ever again in his house or she would be kicked out. Debbie had virtually no choice in the matter whatsoever. She simply had to do what her parents told her she had to do.

As Debbie told me this story and other graphic details, I could feel the pain in her voice. I wanted to hug her, but since we were on the telephone all I could do was listen and give her reassuring remarks. "Oh how cruel, I'm sorry, that must have been terrible!" I said. Growing up literally right across the street from her, I never knew that she was forced to do this. At that time I was only 13 and was oblivious to it. It was something that we did not talk about in our home either. That was the difference between 1968 and 2007.

Debbie continued telling me the horror story of how the nuns took the baby, they held up a sheet so she could not see her baby, hold it or hug it; I had a huge lump in my throat. It seems back in 1968 the psychologists and social workers said it would be best for the baby not to bond with the birth mom. How cruel. How insensitive. What about the mom? I could not imagine the pain Debbie must have felt. I told Debbie that she was one of my new heroes for going through what she did. She gave her son life! She was a light burning in the darkness. She did the right thing. The Lord Jesus was proud of her. I reassured her and realized how blessed I was to be able to get this perspective from her. I also thanked God privately that Mollie was from a different time and place and a different family. Debbie's story gave me courage to realize I must not be like my uncle.

She accepted the consequences of her decision. Even though Debbie's consequences were all given to her and not all chosen by her, she did accept them. Then when I finally asked her for her advice, she gave me the best advice that any father can give to his teenage daughter. She said, "Dick, all I know is that I was made to feel ashamed and guilty. I had literally no say in any of the decisions." Whatever you do, "Let her make all the decisions herself." Tell her the consequences of each decision the best you can. She said, "Explain things to her, but in the end let all the decisions be hers and don't make her feel ashamed." She went on to say, "Love her, Dick, as God has loved you." These were profound words. The best words and the best advice I received was from my own blood relative who had been in Mollie's position some forty years earlier. Now Debbie was fifty three years old, has never been married, and she never had another child. She battled alcoholism addictions and depression. I suddenly saw that I really did not have it that bad. Debbie was right! I had to love Mollie as God loves us all. I had to let her make the decisions. But what about all the consequences to the choices? I did not know what they were much less was I an authority on all these subjects.

I reached out unashamed in confidence and spoke to numerous people for advice. We met with our former pastor whom Linda and I both loved and trusted, Father George Charnley. He mainly listened, but got us hooked up with a catholic counselor who specialized in teenage pregnancy consultation.

We took Mollie and ourselves there for a couple of visits. I think it helped a little. I also decided to tell each of my children, brothers, sisters, and my own Dad in person. I felt it was very important that I be there in front of them to give them "The News." Each of them was very helpful and understanding. I reached out to other friends at work and my Men's Faith Sharing Group from church. The one thing I can tell any family who goes through this, don't be afraid or ashamed to reach out to people whom you can trust. All these people listened and helped me through the entire journey. As a father, you are supposed to be the leader, the tough guy, the person who can fix it all and make all the pain go away. Sometimes though, you simply can't. Sometimes the pain is a good thing that you need so you can grow and learn to trust. So as fathers we tend to hold everything in and the internalization can be very harmful. Reach out to your circle of those you trust and Buckle Your Chin Strap with the Lord. He will help you through each step of the journey just like he did me.

One lesson I learned from my college football playing days is that within a game of football, you will be confronted with "sudden changes." Your team may be on the opponent's 5-yard line going in to score a go ahead touchdown when suddenly the running back fumbles. The fumble is picked up by the opposing team and returned 95 yards for a touchdown for the other team. "Suddenly" the game is changed. This actually did happen in one of our college football games. Our college coach, Jim Harkema, had lectured us many times about sudden changes that will occur in a football game. The point of the matter was not if, but when they do happen, how will our team respond? In football games, these sudden changes happen all the time.

No matter how hard you try to control the game plan, the other team does things to change your circumstances. Instead of scoring the go ahead touchdown and seizing control of the ballgame, you can suddenly find yourself down by two scores. How are you going to react when you are confronted with the adversity of sudden changes?

Coach Jim Harkema taught us this valuable lesson, and it carries over to your living of your life. Although life is not a game, it does have "sudden changes" like the change of a teenage daughter becoming pregnant. Linda and I were supposed to be moving towards the golden years where we could enjoy finally having time with each other.

Our grandchildren would come after our children got married. Right? That was the game plan that we had scripted. But that is not what happened. God had different plans for our lives. It was a "sudden change." I knew deep inside my soul that with God's help, I could "Buckle My Chin Strap" and battle through this sudden change, too. Thankfully, the Lord helped me remember this lesson on sudden change, and He helped me buckle my chin strap securely for enduring all the steps in the journey as a pregnant teenager's father. The journey was going to be tough. But how tough it would be was beyond my wildest imagination. Soon I would learn just how tough each step would be.

*Luke Chapter 14 Verse 26*
*"Whoever does not carry his own cross and come after me cannot be my disciple."*

This verse says it all. All of us who journey in this earthly vessel will be confronted with "News," challenges, or problems in our lives. When we receive these "bumps in the road" as I like to call them, what will we do? Will we focus on the "bump" or the journey? Will we look at the forest or the trees? Jesus carried His and our cross after being scourged, whipped and tormented. Even the Lord Jesus Himself fell three times while carrying His cross! Do you not think He could have called His Fathers' angels to help carry the cross the remainder of His journey if He had wanted? Instead, He chose to try and carry it Himself in His torn and shattered earthly body. After falling a third time, what happened? He got help from Simon of Cyrene to carry the cross the rest of his journey. Even our Lord got help. We too must "try our best" to carry our crosses in life. They will surely come. But when they get too heavy to carry and they will, look to the Holy Spirit and to those around you for help.

If you Buckle Your Chin Strap with the Holy Spirit you can carry any cross. The secret to this journey is to focus on each step, one step at a time. Through the grace of the Holy Spirit and my family and friends who were in fact Simon of Cyrene to me, I was able to withstand the news and the journey. I am carrying my cross and I am helping Mollie carry hers, too.

# Chapter 3
## Decision Time

*Isaiah Chapter 26 Verse 4*
*"Trust in the Lord Forever! For the Lord is an eternal rock."*

When you have to make an important decision in your life, what do you do? How do you know that what you decide will work out or not? What will the outcome be of your choice? How will it affect your life and the lives of those whom you love? These are the questions any of us face when we are confronted with the really monumental decisions in our lives. This is what my daughter faced when she had to make the decision of what to do with her pregnancy, and her child. As a father, one of the most difficult things was that I could not make this decision for her. She had to make it. I had to have faith that I brought her up well enough to make the right decision. We raised all of our children to know that two wrongs don't make a right. Mollie knew in her heart what was right as do most women and girls when it comes to childbirth.

I had to trust in the Lord. I buckled my chin strap in faith that He would give me His words to say to my daughter. I trusted in the Lord that His Holy Spirit would give me these words and I did not worry what I would say or how to say them because I knew the Lord was my eternal ROCK. I trusted in the Lord that his Holy Spirit would not only guide me, but more importantly guide her. He is and was our eternal rock. The next time you have to make an important life changing decision remember that if you trust in Him,

He will be your eternal rock. Don't worry about the outcome. He is already there.

On the fourth day of our "hunkering down" at home, it became apparent that we needed to face reality. We could not hide away in our home with the phone off the hook, watching old movies and pretending nothing was wrong forever. We needed to confront the problem head on. We could not ignore the fact that a decision had to be made.

As a father, this was probably one of the most difficult steps if not the most difficult in the journey. For me, I wanted to fix it and make it all better, but this was not my decision to make. By now, I had received all types of advice from close friends, our pastor, my cousin Debbie, lawyers, and counselors on what to do. My wife Linda and I had to discuss how we were going to proceed with this decision. I knew in my heart that abortion was wrong. I knew that it was murdering an innocent child. I had always said I was against abortion and was pro-life, but now the pro-life versus abortion dilemma was too close for comfort! Pro-life versus abortion was not only in my neighborhood or backyard; it was in my own house! What was I going to do?

Satan is a great deceiver. In times of your most challenging weakness he comes in the strongest. He tries to get you to rationalize that the easy way is the best way. Take the road this way and all this will be in your rear view mirror. Go ahead tell her she needs to get an abortion and all this will be over. It will be done. This situation will be over and out of your life. It will be as if nothing ever happened. After all, an abortion is "just science, use science to solve the problem. Go ahead, tell her to get an abortion. While you are at it, demand that she get an abortion, it will be the best thing for her and you and your family. It will be okay. God will understand and He will forgive you." These are the thoughts that the greatest deceiver of all time puts into your head and into the heads of others who are close to you. Prepare yourself for these deceivers.

Some of those closest to me actually made comments to me that this would be what we should do. I knew that their intentions were based on their love for Mollie and us, how ill-confused they must have been. They all said that God would forgive this sin. He forgives all sin and this would be the best thing for our daughter. God will understand. She would get to go away to college. She would be able to live the normal life as a high school teenager. Her dreams would be able to be realized. She would not be sentenced to a life of struggle, misery and failure. But would she really if she chose this path? Thankfully, the "Holy Spirit" is a greater defender, than Satan is as a deceiver. I told those who told me these things to essentially get behind me you Satans. I am the Lord's son and I will not compromise my faith to encourage her to take the easy road. As for me and my house, we will serve the Lord. I told them that if they wanted me to kill my grandchild, they should go out and buy a gun, shoot me in the head and kill me when I am defenseless in my sleep.

When you abort a baby that is essentially what you are doing. You are killing someone who is defenseless. Abortion is murder. I told them that after they kill me, they could go ahead and kill my grandchild next. Then they could live with the consequences. After I told a few of the well meaning deceivers this, they shut right up because they knew I was right. It really was not me who said these words, as they came from the Lord. They came from my great defender, the same Lord who defended each and every one of us at Calvary. There was no way I could sign papers to approve of my daughter murdering my own flesh and blood, let alone the fact that there was already a soul growing in her womb. A soul that God already knew and put there to be born.

However, as my wife Linda and I discussed this in our bedroom for hours at nauseam, away from Mollie, we both agreed that "the decision" was not ours to make. The decision, as counseled by my cousin Debbie, should rightfully be our daughter's. After all, it was her life, her future, and her baby. Although the decision would affect Linda and me, we knew as Debbie counseled, "Let her make all the decisions" was the right thing to do. "But how could a 16 year old make this decision?" Mollie was not 16 going on 21 as her older sister Amber was at that age. Being our youngest child, we had babied her. She was actually more like 13 or 14 in terms of her maturity. But all this perception would soon change, too. We would be surprised to learn just how mature she really was upon our presentation of "the decision time" to her.

As I prepared to present the decision options to her, my gut wrenched with turmoil. For the past 26 years, I had worked for the same company in a variety of sales positions. I was used to presenting concepts, ideas and proposals to customers. But Mollie was more than a prospective customer. The child growing in her womb was not a product or service to sell. How could I present the decision options and their consequences when I had no understanding how they would truly impact her, her future life or ours? Once again, I buckled my chin strap with the Lord.

I recalled the spring semester of 1979, my senior year of college. As a 21 year old young man, I was confronted with another life changing decision that had to be made. This time the decision was all mine. I was five years older than Mollie and at the time it was the most difficult decision I had ever had to make. By no means though did it have the level of potential life changing conflict that Mollie's decision had. Nonetheless, it was a learning reflection the Lord provided.

I had just finished my senior year of college football at GVSU. We had a terrific season and finished 10-3 losing in the National Semifinal Playoff game. We won our league championship. We lost 13-7 to Elon College in North Carolina in a deluge of non-stop heavy rain in the worst field conditions I have ever seen or played in all my years of football. The team would only lose six starters off that team going into the fall of 1979. However, they would only lose five, if I decided to come back and play a 5th year. After my sophomore season, I had hurt my knee in spring football practice and had a torn MCL (Medial Collateral Ligament) surgery to repair my knee. After consulting my doctor and our athletic trainer the fall of my junior year, I decided that my knee was not ready yet and I needed to spend that entire year rehabilitating and strengthening it. So I missed my entire junior season due to the knee injury.

In that spring of 1979 I had to make a decision. Did I want to come back and play a fifth year or should I graduate? All my closest friends were graduating. I could graduate, too, if I wanted. However, if I chose to come back and play a fifth year, I would have to take a couple classes that did not count towards my major and graduation requirements during that upcoming 1979 spring term. The NCAA rules back then required that you had to not only have a year of eligibility left due to injury or transfers, but you needed to have academic classes you needed to fulfill as well. If I had fulfilled all of my academic requirements to get my degree, the NCAA would have ruled me ineligible even though I had really only played and competed for three seasons. It would not have mattered. I still needed three business classes to graduate, and if not, the NCAA would not have let me come back and play a fifth year via the NCAA rules. It was a difficult decision for me at the time.

My coaches wanted me to come back. My returning teammates wanted me to come back. I think my parents wanted me to play another year, but they simply told me the decision was mine to make. My younger brother Dave wanted me to come back. He was actually two years younger than me. He had followed me to Grand Valley State in the fall of 1977 which was my junior season. This was the season I sat out due to my knee surgery. My senior season of 1978, Dave started at left guard and I started also once again at right guard on the offensive line. It was very special to finally play with my brother and be the "Williams Brothers" guard team. My parents were very proud and I secretly was, too. My brother and I were close even though as children growing up we had our share of spats and sibling rivalry. I was his big bro and the two of us were the "pulling guards" from Jackson Lumen Christi. The Williams Brothers who could put a charge into any linebacker or defensive cornerback trying to knife a sweep.

Even in 1979, I knew the Lord thanks to my Catholic upbringing and twelve years of catholic education given to me by loving mom and dad. I prayed to the Lord. I asked the Lord for the guidance in what to do. I asked him to light my path. Guide my steps Lord and tell me what I should do. I wanted to get a job and gain some "material world" things like a car, apartment, and stereo, etc. Things I could not afford while in college. It was a difficult decision.

One night approximately two days before the registration for spring semester classes ended, my prayers were answered. It was probably 2:30am or so and after tossing and turning I could not sleep. I got up, went downstairs into the green cove where our bean bag chair resided and put my roommate's stereo and headphones on to listen to the radio. While listening, I heard a song come on the radio entitled "I'll Play for You." The artists were Seals and Croft, a popular folk band back in the mid 1970s. As I listened to the words of that song, I knew what the Lord had called me to do. The words to the song were as follows:

*"Tonight while the lights are shining and the microphone is on, I'll play for you. So many will be the blessings and so short will the time, I'll stay with you. But I'll play for, I love you yes I do. You can say that I'm your friend, you can see my life begin and end, I'll always play for you.*

*Hear the band, hear the band. Won't you let the music take you, hear the band. And let this night go on forever, and don't you ever stop the music, let your spirit set you free.*

*Hear the band, hear the band. You can sing and stomp your feet and clap your hands and these few moments we'll share together, and I'll play for you.*

*I've practiced many years and I have come a long, long way just to play for you. My life is but a song that I have written in many ways, just to say to you. To say, I love you yes I do. And I'd like for you to be whatever you would like to be, you'll always be special to me."*

Wow! Did these lyrics ever speak to my heart on that long ago early morning/late evening in the winter of 1979. The words hit me like a strong safety smack in the mouth. I knew in an instant that the Lord was telling me to play for Him. I knew that He was telling me to, "Come back and play" one more year. So I promptly informed my coaches, my teammates and family of my decision that next morning and registered for spring term classes with one day to spare. The classes I registered for were what we used to term as "blow off" or very easy classes, since I had all my requirements taken but three business classes, I saved them for the following fall.

Let's just say that the spring of 1979 featured many non-traditional spring terms for a normal college student athlete who played football. I had a lot of late nights which were spent not studying, frequent trips to the golf courses, and Lake Michigan along with spring football practice that last spring term. It was probably the most fun I had in my four years of college.

The following fall of 1979, the year I came back to play as a red-shirt season, much to my dismay was a major letdown. The team's record was a dismal five wins and five losses. We lost four of our five games by five or less points. We were a bull's eye on everyone's schedule due to the year before in which we had our exceptional season and playoff run to the National Semi-Final Game. Literally every team we played had us circled on their schedule to give it their best effort. Most of the teams did exactly that, too. Some games we played down to a lower level, but most teams just got fired up to try and beat us. I only got to play in 5 of our 10 games due to constant re-aggravation and injury to my surgically repaired left knee.

At the time, it was one of the most frustrating experiences in my athletic career. How could this be happening? My knee had been perfect all last season and through spring football practice. Why was the Lord allowing constant re-injury of this leg? Hadn't I been an obedient son? I listened to you Lord and came back to play one more year for you. How could this happen? Why are you doing this to me? Why are we losing all these close games? These are the types of questions I remember posing or should I say shouting to our Lord back in the fall of 1979. Not until some years later, did I realize how God would bless, reward and discipline me for listening to Him and coming back.

The night of the last game of my football career a game we lost 14-9; I was leaving a late night party to walk home early as my friends stayed and partied. I was feeling sorry for myself, disappointed with my teammates and regretting my decision to come back. I remember thinking all my personal goals were left unattained. No national championship, no all league honors would come my way due to missing so many games, no Academic All-American honors would come my way due to missed competitions. No recognition would come after all my years of hard work, perseverance and dedication. It seemed like I had made a big mistake!

As I was mulling these thoughts over in my mind, I was walking aimlessly through a dark parking lot in the Campus View Apartment complex to make my way back to my apartment, which was about a half-mile walk if you cut through all the parking lots.

Suddenly, I heard a woman's voice say, "Dick, is that you Dick Williams?" I looked up and quickly had all my negative thoughts vanish. The woman who stood before me was Linda Gates, the most beautiful girl I had ever laid eyes on, was standing before me! She had been at a different party that night visiting a couple of her friends and was leaving to get into her car. What a coincidence and good fortune that was. I had met Linda and became really good friends with her some two and a half years earlier. We had not seen each other in approximately a year. She had dated the fullback on our team who graduated and had broken up with him about a year and half earlier and then she left school. I had longed to see her again, but did not know her telephone number or how to reach her. Linda and I small talked in the parking lot for 10 or 15 minutes and then she offered to give me a ride to wherever I was going. She knew I was car-less and a poor jock. I graciously accepted her offer and in no time she was parked directly in front of Ravine 17 which was my apartment complex. Feeling the effects of a long season and a few beverages to drown my sorrows that evening at the party, I mustered some rarely found courage to ask her out on a date. I only had one other girlfriend in my entire life from high school and because I had no car, I never asked any girls out for dates. I asked her for dinner and a movie for that following Saturday night.

As I asked her out for our first date, I imagined to myself, "Oh, she probably has a serious boyfriend by now, and she will say thanks, but no thanks. Since I had only dated one other girl in high school and my first year in college, I had very low self esteem and confidence when it came to asking girls out. Yes believe it or not, I was shy. To my surprise, she accepted and from that moment on the rest was history. We dated from the fall of 1979 until the fall of 1980 where I promptly proposed and we were married a half year later on a brilliant 73 degree sunny day May 2, 1981 in St. Andrews Cathedral in Grand Rapids, Michigan, by my high school principal Father Joseph Coyle, another great man in my life.

Now looking back, I know why God wanted me to come back and play for him. He wanted to reward and bless me with my bride and soulmate Linda. If I had not listened to Him and graduated instead, who knows where I'd be, who knows who I would be and how I would be today. Linda is my soulmate, my best friend and is the best blessing God has ever given to me. I thank Him every day for her. I truly believe that He would have blessed me even more, had I truly made the decision entirely to "Play for Him." The personal and selfish goals I had that were not accomplished due to repeated re-aggravation of my MCL knee injury was all God's way of disciplining me. He was showing me at the time that I needed to commit total trust and be unselfish. That was and still is a hard thing for me and I believe any of us to do. Totally trust in the Lord and let Him direct your path.

Reflecting on this important decision I made gave me insight in how to properly present the decision options to Mollie. I told her this story and how the decision affected me and her mother and literally everyone she knows including herself. I told her that although none of us have a crystal ball to see what the future holds, not to fear because, you should trust in the Lord. She saw first hand what my decision had done for me and her life, and it was a good bridge into what will most likely be one of her most difficult decisions she ever makes in her lifetime.

As we started the discussion on her decision options, I prefaced her by telling her that we were going to explain the four options she had, and that the decision was hers to make. She could change her mind and she could ask for any advice or counsel from us or anyone she wanted, but that we would explain the "pros and cons" the best we could of each option.

I began with the abortion option. How could I start with this option you may ask? Aren't you a Christian father, a Christian man? Why are you telling her that this is even an option? Are you some type of hypocrite? Many of these types of questions went through my mind as well. But if we did not tell her this was one of her options, her friends and others would. She needed to hear it from us first and from a Godly Christian perspective. I began by saying, "Your first option is to choose an abortion. An abortion is where a mother and father choose to intentionally murder their unborn, defenseless baby which is alive and growing in the mother's womb."

The good thing about an abortion is that this whole thing can be over! To everyone up at the high school, you will still be Mollie Williams on the outside. You won't have to worry about kids whispering about you or pointing at your stomach as you walk the hallways pregnant. You won't have to feel the pains of morning sickness any longer; you won't have to feel the pains of childbirth. Monetarily, your life will not be taxed with the early responsibilities of feeding, clothing, and caring for your baby. You won't have to give up the normal activities of your junior and senior years of high school and going away to college dreams. It will be as if none of this has happened! A time warp! You can pretend to everyone else, that all is fine and dandy. These were all the pros to having an abortion that I could think of.

Next came the cons. "But Mollie as you know, with every decision you make there are also cons that can adversely affect you and even haunt you for years to come. If you get an abortion, you will have to live with the fact that you murdered your defenseless child, killing him or her because you desired to take no responsibility for your actions. If you get an abortion, not only will these thoughts haunt you, but you may not even be able to have another child. Abortion affects a woman's ability to conceive in the future and you could possibly never have another child again. Additionally, you will have to tell your husband this if you get married and if you cannot conceive because of the abortion, it may affect your relationship with your husband. So Mollie, if you think you can live with the abortion, pick the abortion and murder your unborn child."

I had to have faith in God that Linda and I had raised her right and prayed that she would not have picked this option. At 16 years of age, there is no way I would have signed for an abortion. In our state, as is the case in other states, if you are not an adult, the parents have to sign consent to the abortion. If Mollie had picked this option I would not have known what to do, except maybe take her to counselors and ultrasounds of the baby etc. so she could really become totally educated on the insanity that would have been inherent in this choice. I had asked God to give me the words to say to Mollie and He did.

The second option I presented to Mollie was adoption. "Mollie," I began, "a second option for you would be to carry the baby and give him or her the gift of life to a married set of parents in the way of an adoption." The good thing about adoption is that you would be accepting responsibility for your actions. Another good thing about an adoption is that you would be giving a gift to a family who might not ever be able to have a child of their own. You would be able to return to high school in your junior and senior year and complete high school without the responsibilities of being a parent. You could continue cheerleading and still enjoy all the sporting events and other high school activities without the hassle and worry of being a mom. Also, you will be able to pursue your dream of becoming a nurse and go away to college.

I went on to tell her that if she chose adoption she was lucky because there were two types of adoption to consider. Traditional adoption or "closed" and progressive adoption or "open." Closed adoptions are where you would simply register with an adoption agency and the parents would be chosen by the adoption agency via their criteria. You would give your baby away and not have any further contact with the child. It would be as if the whole event was some kind of a dream or nightmare. You could go on living a normal teenager's life after giving birth.

The open adoption would be much different. In an open adoption, the mother and father essentially create a contract with the perspective parents and draft their requirements of the terms of giving their child away. They could ask for quarterly visits, Christmas visits, pictures every month, telephone calls weekly with updates, whatever her and the father would want. They also would get to interview and choose the parents for their child. It would be a tough process to go through and it could be reassuring to stay involved in the baby's life. Thankfully, I knew a lot about this option. Our dear friends Don and Judy Strock with whom we had spent our Hawaiian 25th wedding anniversary/second honeymoon together, had a daughter who chose this option after a pregnancy while a sophomore in college. I told Mollie that we could arrange a meeting with her and Katie Strock, our friend's daughter, so she could talk with her about this option. Mollie did arrange the meeting with Katie and she spent an entire afternoon with her discussing how a progressive open adoption worked for her. We let Mollie do this alone with Katie without us clamoring over every dilemma or imposing on the questions she asked. Katie was a very good friend and an even better Christian girl. We were thankful to have had this resource to help Mollie.

"But Mollie, as with abortion, adoption also has some cons or negative consequences. First, you may never be able to have another child again. This may be your only child and you could possibly be giving away your only chance to ever experience the joy of being a mother. Secondly, your mind will constantly wonder; what is my child doing today? Every holiday from Christmas to Valentine's, to Easter to Memorial Day, to Halloween and Thanksgiving, your arms will long to hold your child. You will have to be able to live with these constant thoughts of where is my child, what is my child doing now, and should I really have given him or her away?" Once again I was blessed to have gotten all these negative consequences or the cons from my cousin Debbie who some 40 years earlier had been forced by her dad to give her son up for an adoption. What a nightmare she had to live everyday experiencing these thoughts. Debbie had also told me that two weeks after delivering her baby, she had to go to her brother's wife's baby shower for the first "legitimate" grandchild and pretend to be happy. Can you imagine that? She had to attend the shower pretending to be excited for her brother's wife as she was giving my aunt and uncle their first "legitimate" grandchild. As she unwrapped all the outfits, the baby toys, the walkers, the cradles, etc., Debbie had to sit there and ponder why couldn't this have been done for me? How come my baby could never have had a baby shower like this? Why is my baby any less legitimate than my brother's?

Weeks later when Heather was born to my cousin Mike and his wife Connie, Debbie had to attend the baptism and again endure these feelings, thoughts and was tortured by these questions she could never ask, much less get answered. Every holiday that came and went more of those haunting feelings and questions would come. Debbie endured this throughout the birth of six of her nieces and nephews silently enduring the pain. Never being allowed to share it with anyone. She was indeed the queen of Hamilton Street and is still the toughest person in the neighborhood. I know from this newfound context though, that she was not only tough outside, she was strong inside. Once she poured open these stories to me, I listened with a heavy heart and I now have a profound respect for the courage she showed and the pain she has endured throughout most of her life. Without her courage to tell me her story, I would never have been able to share these negative consequences and perspective with Mollie.

I went on, "Now Mollie, society says that giving up your baby to adoption is the "best" thing you can do for the baby and for yourself, but you need to ask yourself, is it really best?" "The divorce rate in America is over 50%. That means you have a 50% chance of picking a couple who will stay together and married. Your child may end up in a broken or worse yet, an abusive home. Will this be best for your baby? How will you know if this child will be baptized and introduced to the gift of salvation through faith in Jesus Christ in parental grace?"

"If the parents divorce will the child really be better off? Secondly, what about you? Will you really be better off with the constant bewilderment of where is my baby, what is he or she doing? Is it worth the risk for you to jeopardize your sanity and your child's future including his or her salvation through Jesus?" "Mollie," I elaborated, "These are the cons of giving your baby away to someone else as best as we can tell you. If you think the baby and you will truly be better off with adoption, go ahead and choose adoption."

The last option was the option I secretly and selfishly desired her to pick. I began, "Mollie, this brings us to your fourth and final option, keeping your child." "Keeping your child is good because you will be assuming 100% of the responsibility for your actions. You will be showing your friends, peers and society that although you made a bad decision to engage in premarital sex, you are taking on all of the consequences of that choice by executing your decision to keep him or her. You will never have to go through what my cousin Debbie did in wondering every day where is my child? What is my child doing today? Is my child happy? Is my child healthy? What type of home life does he or she have? Does my child know Jesus yet? Every birthday you will celebrate it with your child, instead of wondering, how is he or she doing today on his or her birthday? On Halloween, you will get to pick out his or her costume and take him or her trick or treating, instead of wondering what did he or she wear this year."

"On Christmas, Easter and all the other holidays, you will get to see and enjoy your child. Mollie, if this child ends up being your one and only child, you will know for the rest of your life that your sacrifice was worth it. Someday if your child marries and has his or her own children, you will get to know your grandchildren. As your child's mom, you will get all the joys and disappointments of raising your child, not someone else. All the decisions that are made to affect your child will be yours. This child will be loved by you better than anyone else."

"However, Mollie, as it is with the two specific "A" (Adoption/Abortion) options, this option too has its cons or negative consequences. Besides enduring the pregnancy, the pains of childbirth and the gossip that you will endure up at your high school, you will endure a life of sacrifice and struggle and quite possibly suffering. You will be sacrificing your life as a normal teenager because you will be the mom. Your mother will "NOT" be the baby's mom. YOU will be the mom. Mom and I have had our children and we will not be the baby's mom and dad. Your Mom will be Grandma and I will be Grandpa. All the nights that your friends will be attending the basketball, football, soccer and baseball games, you will be either home with your baby, or at work. You will need to get a job or two to learn to support your child and learn to juggle the priorities of mom, school and work."

Up until that time Mollie did not have a job. My wife Linda struggled with her getting a job because she knew that we in effect would be performing the mom and dad duties at night when Mollie worked and after school. After discussing this though, we both felt that if we just let her stay home and be a mom with no job, we would be enabling her which would ultimately lead to her collapse and demise in the future. We had to be strong and not make it "EASY" on her, despite our love for her. It was critical that she learn how to juggle all these priorities as we had to learn, if she was to become a self-supportive working mom. (More on this will be shared later).

So we told her up front, that she would have to sacrifice time with the baby to get a job or two to be able to afford the essentials like diapers, formula, clothes, etc. I told her that she would be sacrificing going away to college like her older brother and sister did. She would have to live at home, attend community college or Eastern Michigan University a college 20 minutes away. I told her that she would not get a car from me like I had purchased while her older sister and brother were in high school in eleventh grade. The child would be costing us anywhere from $150 to $250 per week for babysitting while in high school and college. This translates from $600 to $1000 per month that would have to be funded for childcare while she completed school. $600 - $1000 was the estimate I had gotten from talking with younger working parents with whom my wife or I knew. Obviously that monthly expenditure would have been able to purchase a nice car and pay the insurance.

Neither Linda nor I could afford to quit our jobs to stay home and care for the child. We needed our jobs. I told Mollie that many times in her life she will want to buy things for herself or go places or attend events that she would have to decline due to either lack of money or parental responsibilities. "Mollie, you will become #2 and your child will be #1."

"Your life will be hard and possibly a struggle. But Mollie, as I reflect back on the things that mean the most to me in my life, they are not the things that came easy or were given to me. They are the things I had to work for, struggle for with God's grace and sacrifice for in humbleness. Nothing worthwhile comes easy. Nothing truly appreciated comes without blood, sweat and tears. Your life will be extremely hard. Within a year of having the baby, if you keep it, you will mature from a child to an adult quickly bypassing the carefree teenager and college days." "You will be more mature than your brother and sister combined because you will be a mom." None of Mollie's siblings had gotten married or had children of their own. I concluded this long presentation, the most important presentation I have ever made in my life, like this. "Mollie, if you think you can accept the consequences of keeping your child, go ahead and choose that. Mom and I need you to know that we love you and we will help you as long as we physically and financially can. But we are not going to make it easy on you. It would be unfair to you and unfair to your baby."

"The most important thing for you is to pick the choice you feel you can live with best. There will be life changing consequences with any of the four choices. You should not listen to anyone else on what to do. A couple of years ago, you received the Holy Spirit into your heart when you were confirmed in the sacrament of confirmation. The Holy Spirit is in your heart and dwelling within that heart. He will guide you to the decision He and you know is best for you. Your friends will be giving you all kinds of advice. The father of the baby will be telling you what to do. Your brother, sister, mom and I will try to give you advice. However, none of this matters. Do not listen to any of these people. You have the Holy Spirit as your compass and He will guide your heart to make the decision you know is right and you can live with. Pray about your decision."

"Now Mollie, you don't have to make the decision today and you are entitled to change your mind if you would like later, but are you leaning towards any of the four options I explained today?"

I waited patiently for what seemed like two or three minutes before I got a response. In the silence, I studied her face. She was in a place somewhere deep within her soul. There were wrinkles in her forehead and her eyes were squinting as if she was looking into a bright sunshine. I could hear the clock chime on the mantle in our family room, as I waited patiently for her response. The clock was a Christmas present we had given to Linda's mom, Ruth, who was a wonderful mother-in-law and grandma. Ruth had just passed away five months earlier after a long courageous battle with a host of ailments, which included a lung removal, heart bypass surgery, hip replacement, back surgery, osteoporosis, hypertension and cancer. It was as if the clock chime was Ruthie telling me, "Don't worry Dick, Mollie will make the right decision." "I am in her and she is in me." Mollie looks a lot like Ruth looked as a teenager and has a lot of her personality traits. Every time I hear that clock chime since reclaiming it after her death, I think of Ruth. I miss her dearly and she was one of my best friends. We spoke on the telephone at least twice a week as she lived two and a half hours away in Grand Rapids, Michigan, still the nicest town I have ever lived in.

Ruth would have wanted to take the baby's father Johnny James to the butcher shop and perform a de-neutering surgery on him, but there would be no way she would have encouraged Mollie to choose either of the "A" options. I could hear her shouting that the baby in Mollie's womb was part of her blood too, and it was as if the clock chimed in the silence to let me know that. Finally Mollie spoke, "Well -- I think I'll keep it." I thought, "Praise to you Jesus; no murder will occur here and I will be able to sleep easier tonight." You see, all along I had secretly hoped that Mollie would choose keeping her baby. I know how many of you reading this will think that I was being selfish and I admit it. I was being selfish. I do not think I could have lived with either of the "A" (Abortion/Adoption) options. If she had chosen abortion, there is no way I would have signed a parental consent to murder my own flesh and blood.

I would have been in a tremendous pickle. Abortion would have required a lot of counseling and work. I would have had to convince Mollie that abortion really was the wrong option to choose. I had to have faith that Mollie knew what was right and would not kill her child. Time was not on my side with this "A" option either as she was almost two months along. Thankfully she spared me of this unwanted dilemma.

If she would have chosen the other "A" option of adoption, I would have also had a tough time looking myself in the mirror. I remember asking my wife Linda, what if this happens to be our only grandchild, and we are going to let her ship him or her down the road for someone else to raise him or her. How could I ever forgive myself for not stepping up to the plate and helping my daughter, financially, emotionally, spiritually or otherwise to care for our grandchild? Part of that child's blood was Linda and part of it was me. Part of it was Linda's mom and dad and part of it was my parents as well. If she had chosen the open adoption, it would have been even more difficult for me. Every time I saw either pictures of the child, or on the rare occasions an actual face-to-face visit, I would not be able to look the child in the eyes. I would have felt like I betrayed the child and abandoned him or her so I could make my life and Linda's easier. There was no way I wanted either of the "A" options.

I told my wife Linda I would rather only live another 10 or 15 years and help Mollie and our grandchild, even if I have to endure working longer before I retire, or harder, and incur the added stress of a baby in the house knowing my grandchild was ours and that my daughter was happy. I told her I would choose this option rather than living another 40 years and seeing my daughter experience the pain and suffering that my cousin Debbie had to endure. When my life is over here on this earth, I know where I am going and I want our Lord to say not only am I forgiven, but Dick well done my son. It was my job to be selfish and to be the leader.

As Coach Crowley my high school coach told me in the high school speech meeting, "A leader stands out. A leader does what is best for the team. A leader sets examples for his teammates to follow. A leader is not afraid to do the unpopular thing." Yes I was selfish, but this was another time in my life off the gridiron where I could be a leader. The question was would I be the type of a leader that she, my wife and our other children needed? I prayed with all my heart to be that leader. I could lead my daughter, my wife and the rest of my family through this difficult decision time and still have selfish thoughts. It was okay and I truly felt that our dear Lord would understand where I was coming from. My job though was to present the choices. I knew that only through the Grace of God, He would give me the words and the method to communicate it to my daughter. It was and is the most important presentation I have ever made in my life. It taught me to keep trusting in God and believing that His Holy Spirit would work His will.

As I felt the adrenaline of joy surge through my body, I had learned in my career of selling not to show any of this emotion. I remained as stoic, as I could, so not to let Mollie know that the choice she was leaning towards was in fact the choice I had secretly wanted her to make. Some months after the baby was born, I would ask her about this choice and what choice she thought that her mom and dad wanted her to pick. You would be surprised to know what she thought we wanted her to choose. I sure was.

Nevertheless, I had to continue the discussion and ask one more critical question. If she really wanted to choose the option of keeping the baby what was the reasoning? So I asked her, "Okay Mollie why? Why do you want to keep the baby?" Once again, Mollie withdrew deep within her soul for another 60 seconds or so. This time as I studied her face, it almost appeared to have a glow. A slight, but ever present glow. She looked up at me and with big crocodile tears in her eyes, she gave me the right answer. "Because it's mine," she said. "It's MINE." It was one of the most profound, simple, yet intelligent answers I could have ever heard. My little girl barely 16 was a lot smarter than I thought she was. She taught me many things as a father throughout this journey and this reply of hers taught me never to doubt the power of the Lord to work in your children's hearts. He had given her this wisdom to recover from a poor decision and not complicate that decision with another even poorer decision. I am not contending that the second "A" option (adoption) was a poorer decision. I am only indicating that the first "A" option of abortion would have been another poorer decision. She did not take the easy road. She didn't choose to murder her child. She chose to give her baby life, which in the end, was the right decision.

If your teenage daughter should become pregnant and decision time comes for her, I pray that you will receive God's grace to work for what you pray for. Human nature (when your daughter gets pregnant as a teenager) is to keep it all in. Don't speak with anyone. Don't tell anyone. This is a private family matter. Don't tell anyone. You should be ashamed. Hold it all inside. I believe you should do the opposite. Tell all of the people you are close enough with about it. Seek out their support and trust. If you know women who have had abortions or adoptions or kept their babies as pregnant teens, talk to them. Get their perspectives. But let your daughter make the decision. In the end, if you pray and work for the information to help you and your daughter, God will see to it that your daughter chooses life for her child. I truly believe that no girl ever really wants to murder her child. They are frightened and want to please their parents or boyfriend. If your daughter knows that you will help her and support her, she will make the right decision. The decision that honors God. LIFE!

*Wisdom Chapter 3 Verse 9 – "those who trust in Him shall understand truth and the faithful shall abide with Him in love: because grace and mercy are with His holy ones and His care is with His elect."*

The verses of this chapter focus on trust. When you are blessed with opportunities to make decisions in life, it can be stressful and even gut wrenching. But decisions are really blessings from God in the free will He gave to all of us. The key to making the right decision is to trust in the Lord. If you buckle your chin strap with the Lord in trust, and pray earnestly for Him to guide you in His will, then the correct decision will be made. I believe that there is no way our Lord will let you make the wrong decisions in life if you put your trust in Him. As this verse above says in the book of wisdom, if you trust in Him you will be able to have clear vision to see the truth, and His grace and mercy shall bless you to guide you in your decision making process. I was blessed to learn this early in my life and it helped me in many of my life's decisions. It also helped me in helping my daughter Mollie make the most important decision of her life. For that trust I will be forever grateful to my Lord Jesus Christ.

# Chapter 4
## The Meeting

*Luke Chapter 14 Verse 11*
*"For everyone who exalts himself will be humbled, but the one who humbled himself will be exalted."*

I learned on August 2, 2006, this very lesson of humility. As a family in our community we were highly respected and what you might consider the all-American family. My oldest daughter was a three sport star in high school and homecoming queen. My son Steven was an all around well liked guy by a diverse group of friends in both our community and the community of Western Michigan University, where he was a junior Business School Major. Our son Michael was focused on heavenly missions.

My wife was a teacher at a local elementary school and loved by many families. I had been involved with coaching my children in soccer, baseball, and basketball as they grew up. Mollie was a cheerleader and involved in dance. I had been a choir member in our church since 1988. Life was good and my family was somewhat exalted. When we received "the letter" in the mailbox on August 2, 2006, and subsequently learned of our youngest daughter's pregnancy, we became humbled. It felt like an elevator dropping from the top floor of the Sears Tower in Chicago to the basement in less than a second. It was a great lesson to learn and I am truly thankful that God blessed me with this lesson. This humility would soon be needed as we traveled the rest of Mollie's journey through pregnancy as a teenager.

In fact, one of the first displays of this humility occurred at the meeting of the baby's father and his parents. After we learned of Mollie's pregnancy we had to inquire, "Mollie, do you know who the father is?" She answered that yes, she did as there was only one guy and it was a guy she had met at school named Johnny James. We further asked her, "Have you told him yet?" "No Dad not yet," came her reply. "Well," I said, "you need to tell him and you need to tell his parents, too." This was probably a very difficult thing to do. Mollie had unfortunately only known Johnny for a few weeks and she put herself in a situation where "it" happened. Now she was learning to deal with the consequences of that decision and it would be difficult.

Mollie called Johnny on the telephone and told him the news. She told him that he needed to tell his parents, too. Johnny was at first in a little bit of denial if not a state of shock. No one thinks they will impregnate a teenage girl when they choose to have premarital sex without protection, but it happens alarmingly all too often. I really believe any 18 year old boy would have reacted the same way. It was not as if they had been dating and courting each other for years, it was only weeks. I am sure he was confused, scared and perplexed.

After waiting another week, we once again asked Mollie to find out if Johnny had told his parents. Johnny indicated that he had not told his parents yet. When Mollie proceeded to ask him why not, he gave an answer that gave me insight into a young man whom I had never even met. He told Mollie that his parents owned a furniture store and they worked all year nonstop rarely taking vacations or closing the store. He went on to tell her that they were finally going to go on a vacation in just another week and it would only be for a week. He asked Mollie if it was okay that she wait two weeks before he would tell them. He told Mollie that he did not want to ruin his parents' vacation. That told me that the young man had potential and a good heart, which relieved one of my fears as a father. However, we needed to have a meeting with him and his parents to communicate the situation and time was of the essence. My wife, bless her heart, can be ruthless when one of her children is hurting. She wanted to call them and ruin their vacation. After all, in her way of thinking, their dear son had ruined our daughter's life, why should we care about their vacation? As we discussed this, the verse on humility was ringing in my heart. I knew that we needed to remain humble and let them go on this vacation. I told Linda that this told me a lot about this young man's heart and that he cared enough for his parents to react this way. I asked her, "What was another couple weeks in the scheme of things?" There was no way we would call them yet. However, we told Mollie that if Johnny did not tell them by the Monday of their return from vacation, we were going to call his parents that Tuesday night ourselves. That way she could send the message to Johnny that it was his choice, but he only had a day when they got back.

Johnny's parents' vacation came and went and true to his word he did tell them the news on that Sunday the day they returned home. I am sure it was equally as difficult and shocking on him and them. Johnny told Mollie that next day Monday at school that he had told his parents. We had previously given Mollie the nights that following week which we would be available to meet with him and his parents at our home to discuss the situation. They chose Thursday night at 7:00 p.m. and "the meeting" was on.

As Mollie, Linda and I prepared over the next week for this meeting, the anxiety kept building as each day drew nearer to that Thursday night meeting. My wife was very concerned about what should we say? Should we shake their hands as they come into our home? What if they are still in denial? What if they say they want to do a paternity test? How will we react if they are defensive? Needless to say, neither of us knew each other much less did we know eachother's child. What an awkward and humbling way to meet someone. "Hi there nice to meet you, your son got our daughter pregnant." It was a very humbling experience.

As a salesman, I was very accustomed to meeting new people every day that I did not know, so that part would be relatively easy for me. However, this was once again not a sales meeting. It was a life meeting, one which would lay the foundation as to how our two families would relate to each other and live with Mollie's pregnancy and the eventual baby. Once again, I had to buckle my chin strap with the Lord. I knew that if I prayed earnestly, that He would send His Holy Spirit to me so that I could conduct this meeting. My wife Linda was still a wreck and could be a firecracker and confrontational in these types of situations. I had to seek my wisdom from the Lord. I prayed earnestly every day incessantly for Him to light my path and guide my steps, while maintaining a humble heart.

As I reflected on all the meetings I had in my life, I cannot think of one that had the life-changing ramifications and the awkwardness of this meeting's potential. I did recall though, the meeting I had with Grand Valley State head football coach Jim Harkema back in the spring of 1978 heading into my senior year. This meeting and the collect phone call from Florida that I had to make, was extremely awkward and I was equally scared. That spring, about 10 of my college football teammates and I traveled to Florida's Daytona Beach for our spring break. We rented two rooms and we crammed five to a room. If any of you have ever participated in a spring break, you know the routine. After taking turns driving down there in two cars, we enjoyed the beach, the sun, the discos, and the parties. At age 21 we were all legal to drink alcoholic beverages, as the drinking age was 18 when I was in college. Our coach only had two team rules which indicated what type of person he was. The first rule was to "act like a man and you will be treated like a man, but act as a boy and you will be treated as a boy." His second team rule was "don't do anything to embarrass yourself, your family, your teammates or Grand Valley State University."

The Thursday night two days before we were supposed to leave Daytona Beach for home, we went to several of the local clubs and establishments. We danced with the girls and had a very good time. After the establishments closed, we decided to all go to an IHOP restaurant that was open 24 hours a day. It was late, but we were all starving even though it must have been about 2:30am. We could get a nice breakfast and return to the hotel for a couple hours sleep before we would hit the beach for our last full day of rays.

The IHOP was packed with other college kids who were no doubt in the same mindset and condition that we were in. We had to wait about 20 or 30 minutes before we could get a table for 10 guys. Once we got our table we ordered a feast and quickly began to scarf all the food like we were ravenous lions who had been without a meal for days. As we finished our meals, one of my buddies, who was the strong safety on our team, noticed that a group of the girls we had met earlier that night were just entering the restaurant. All of my teammates decided that they wanted to stay and follow these girls to their hotel, which was on the opposite end of the Daytona Beach strip. I was exhausted and tired and wanted to go back to the room to crash. I tried to convince my teammates to go back with me, but none of them would listen. I did not own a car, so I was left with two options, either walk back to the hotel or stay with the guys. I chose the former despite my exhaustion; I could be stubborn back then, so I started walking. I knew it was almost a 1/2 hour walk, but if I was lucky, I could hitch a ride and be back in five minutes.

Daytona Beach strip at 3:45am was still very active and there were a lot of cars still out cruising. I began walking and told my buddies to have fun, but I was heading back. I was always my own man even back then, and when I make my mind up to do something, I do it. In any event, I started walking. As I got about two blocks from the IHOP, I decided to start "thumbing it" as we called it, to hitch a ride back to the hotel. I was exhausted from the sun, beach and disco fun. I could not wait to get back to the hotel and go to sleep.

Suddenly, out of the corner of my eye, I caught a glimpse of Daytona's finest pulling out from behind a large dumpster directly across the street from where I was hitchhiking. I jumped back up on the sidewalk and continued walking. The police officers turned on their flashers and pulled up behind me. "You there stop in your tracks," I heard on a booming megaphone. "That police officer could not be talking to me," I thought. I had only just started hitchhiking. I had not done anything wrong as far as I knew. I stopped, turned around and pointed to myself, "Are you speaking to me," I yelled. The officers got out of the car. One was a short stocky guy about 5'9" with a flat top haircut and looked like a modern day version of Sargent Carter from the Gomer Pyle show which I watched on television when I was a kid growing up. The other guy was about 6' tall, either of Latino or Mexican decent, skinny and Hollywood looking. They were both probably in their early 30s. They threw me up against their squad car, with the shorter Sargent Carter looking dude trying with all his might to forearm my face up against the side window. I was quite strong from all the weightlifting I had done, and there was no way some police officers were going to physically abuse me. After all, I had done nothing wrong. I resisted the one officer's forearm and he was unable to push my head against the window. I yelled to the officers "look sirs, I have done nothing wrong; I am just on my way back to the hotel." I think the officers were bored and had decided to have fun with a college kid to see if they could earn some points for arresting another spring break punk.

As the officers saw I was somewhat strong, they were not going to get too physical with me so I just put my hands on their car windows and spread my legs. They frisked me as if I would be carrying a gun or concealed weapon. Finally, they put handcuffs on me behind my back and made me stand in front of their squad car for another five or ten minutes as the two of them went back into their car to look me up on their system.

Back then, they would call my license into dispatch and have their dispatch person enter my license into their large main frame computer system. They found no record or problems and came back out of their squad cars. "Finally!" I thought, as I waited for what seemed like a half hour but was actually only five minutes or so. I immediately asked the one taller slender officer who had the Latino/Mexican Hollywood look, "Sir, could you tell me for what reason I am being detained?" He would only say you know why son and then laughed to his partner. I waited for another five or ten minutes in front of their squad car with their flashers blazing and their spotlight right in my eyes. I could barely see as it was extremely bright.

Soon a paddy wagon pulled up and I was shoved inside the paddy wagon.

I was being arrested, but what crime had I committed? I had understood that hitchhiking in the city limits was legal as I saw many other kids doing it over the past week while I was there. I once again implored the officers as they tried to shove me in the wagon, Sirs please tell me what I am being arrested for. They would not respond, they only laughed and said that I would find out soon enough.

The next few hours were the longest hours of my life up until that time. I learned something I wished I never had to learn about the criminal justice system and myself in those hours. I first learned that the criminal justice system has police officers who are unfortunately corrupt. But more importantly, I learned that there was no way I ever wanted to spend another night in jail.

The paddy wagon was a big black truck similar to a UPS truck. Once inside, it had two long steel benches down each side of the vehicle so that prisoners faced each other while enjoying their ride to insanity. The rear of the truck had two small windows about 2' x 2' with steel cast iron bars spaced every three or four inches. As I sat inside the paddy wagon and peered out one of these tiny windows, I thought to myself, "What is happening? Why did they arrest me? Where are they taking me?" The paddy wagon made three or four other stops to pick up other college kids on its way to a local county fairgrounds.

When we arrived at the fairgrounds, there were portable lights set up along with three or four circus style tents. Each tent was set up in an assembly line fashion with two lines to enter and two lines for exiting. There were at least 50 to 60 other college kids waiting in line. Each line had police officers seated at tables which checked in all of your valuables. It appeared to me that they had a production line to make money for the local community at college kids' expense. As I got in line, I felt as low as I have ever felt in my life.

Now I know what the Lamb heading into a slaughterhouse felt like. I was arrested it appeared for hitchhiking. What was going to happen? How long was I going to be in jail? What was I going to do? How would I tell my parents? Who would I call with my one phone call? Several of these questions raced through my mind.

Once I got into the jail cell I was appalled. There were only three large holding cells each designed for maybe fifty people at most but each was crammed with eighty to one hundred other college kids. There was one toilet made of steel and about eight or ten bunk beds. Each of the three cells had at least eighty to one hundred guys inside and they were standing shoulder to shoulder crammed in like sardines. You could hardly move. The smell of the jail was that of the worst body odors, alcohol, smoke combination that to this day I have ever smelled. It was a scary and humiliating experience.

Some guys were sitting on the floor sleeping. Some were lucky enough to get one of the bunk beds. I was shoved into the first cell and made my way to a corner in the front near the door. I had made my mind up that I would speak to no one, nor would I utter even one word. Several guys tried to get me to talk. I just shut it down and tried to remain alert and calm, despite the conditions. As I stood in the corner it was now about 6:00am and I thought of how St. John and St. Paul were both wrongly imprisoned for their faith and how they endured their plights. I now knew a little of what they went through, even if it was only a fraction of their experiences.

About 8:50am the bailiff opened our cells and escorted us over to the courtroom. The courtroom was a separate building and they were connected by a long narrow dimly lit hallway with no windows. The hallway was dark and made of cinder block construction although it was painted white. It was about 30 to 40 yards long. We were all escorted to the back of a large courtroom where many of us stood throughout the entire proceeding. There were at least 250 to 300 of us college kids jammed into this courtroom along with others there for larceny, assaults, felonies, traffic fines, domestic disputes, etc. We all sat or stood. Fortunately for me, since I was one of the last in, I was near the door and one of the first out of the cell. I was able to sit in one of the chairs. It never felt so good to sit in my life. After a long night, I was exhausted and just thankful to finally sit in a chair albeit made of hard dark oak wood; it was a welcome sight.

After waiting about ten minutes, the judge finally came into the courtroom. He must've been in his late 50s or early 60s. He had slightly graying hair, wore bifocal large wire-rimmed glasses and wore a stern and confident frown on his face. He first went through all of the felony cases such as larceny, assault, domestic disputes, and then the traffic cases. That took about an hour or so. After he had finished these cases, he arrogantly announced, "Okay, everyone I am going to call now is being charged with open containers of alcohol in public or on the beach. You may plead guilty and receive the time served in jail last night and a $26 fine; or you may plead not guilty and post a $50 bond at which point we will set a trial date." I remember thinking to myself, "Wow that sure is a stiff fine for drinking." I quickly did the math and estimated that it was a nice way to make their community $7,000 to $8,000 a night. I was sure glad all I did was hitchhike.

The judge proceeded to call out names for the next 20 minutes at which point every college kid pled guilty and took the night in jail with a $26 fine. Everyone was tired and just wanted out of there. As the judge rolled through the names, he would call some people by only their last name such as Tarrant, Beaudrie or Thompson. But most of the time when he called out someone's name, he would do so by calling their full legal name Joseph Pollard, James Grignon, Frank Yesh, etc. I was starting to get sleepy and almost delirious as the judge called through the names. Finally, I heard him say, in his authoritative voice, "Williams." I instantly received a wake-up call or shot of adrenaline and sat up in my chair. Since the judge had said everyone he was going to call was guilty of open containers, I did not say anything as I was guilty of hitchhiking, not open containers of alcohol. I remember thinking to myself at the time, with three hundred college kids and with my common last name of Williams, "Chances are high that some other kid here has the same last name as mine." I remained silent. Once again the judge shouted, "Williams!" I stayed silent. "Surely it was someone else," I thought. He mumbled something like, "I will assume silence means you are pleading not guilty and will set a trial date for May 13th and you must post the $50 bond." After the judge finished his last open container plea, he suddenly took his gavel, pounded it twice on his desk and said, "I hope you kids learn your lesson that we in Daytona do not want our beaches covered with alcohol and walking the streets with open containers in public. Enjoy the rest of your stay and please do not let me see you here again." Then he slammed the gavel down one more time and announced, "Court is adjourned."

He never got to my case. "Was he just taking a break?" I wondered, "Was he going to come back and get to my case?" "Were there others there too who had not had their names called?" I jumped up immediately and yelled, "Excuse me your honor," and raced towards the bench. I was promptly greeted by two or three court officers who grabbed me and made a wall between the judge's exit door and the bench. As I saw the judge leave the courtroom, I began to frantically ask these court officers, "Sirs, is he coming back into the courtroom in a few minutes after a break or is court adjourned for the day?" One of the officers who was probably 45 or 50 years old with kind eyes, medium build and about my height 6'3" looked me in the eyes and said, "No, son, he is done for the day." I started to tell this officer the story about hitchhiking and why I had been arrested. He asked me to sit down for a minute while he and the rest of the officers cleared the courtroom of all the college kids. He said he would come back in five minutes or so and help me clear this up. Well, five minutes turned into at least 15 or 20. I waited there in handcuffs, exhausted and ashamed thinking bitterly to myself, "how could this be happening?" "What was going to happen now? Was I going to be forced to spend the rest of the weekend in jail?" This is totally unfair. The judge had called my last name for a crime I did not commit, and to make matters worse, we were supposed to leave Saturday morning to drive back to Grand Rapids, Michigan.

It will be a 21 hour trek in order to be there in time for classes on Monday and the start of spring football practice. How could this be happening? What was I going to tell Coach Harkema? How would I get home if I had to spend the weekend in jail? What will my teammates do? If they left me, I would be alone, five states south of home and virtually broke. I only had about $35 left. Finally after the long wait, the officer returned to the courtroom. I told him once again why I was arrested. The judge had said, "Everyone whose name I call was guilty of open containers of alcohol in public," and I had been arrested for hitchhiking not open container. I told him further how the judge had only called out the last name of "Williams," not my full name, which was why I had remained silent. This officer was the first kind officer I had met, and I could tell that he was sympathetic and actually he apologized for the mix-up. He got out the court records, found my name and confirmed that yes, I had been written up for open container. I asked the officer if hitchhiking was a crime and he, too, would not give me a straight answer. All he said was, "Wait here for another minute son, I will go and get the judge and we will clear this matter up." All along my suspicions had been correct, the officers who arrested me were bored and had their fun with me, because I looked like a drunken college kid who thought that hitchhiking may have been illegal.

The fact is, as I learned from a college friend's father some months later, that hitchhiking was not illegal inside the city limits of Daytona Beach. These officers had falsely arrested me and wrote me up for a crime I did not commit because they were either below their quotas, or were bored. I felt like a victim. But I knew I had to get out of there. By now it was almost noon and I still had time to get back to the hotel, shower and grab a couple hours sleep before the last night in Daytona. I could hardly wait for the officer and the judge to return. After about five minutes, the officer returned and grimly announced that unfortunately, the judge had left the courthouse for the weekend and would not return until Monday. "Monday," I exclaimed! "What do you mean Monday? I have to get back to Michigan. I have to leave tomorrow morning. We start college football practice on Monday and I have nine teammates back at the hotel waiting for me." "What was I supposed to do?" I thought, "Here I was being forced to stay until Monday to clear up an error for a crime I did not commit." It took a great deal of composure as tired as I was, but I calmly asked the officer if I could be released until Monday. He looked at me solemnly with his kind eyes and said, "No son, you have to post a $50 bond to get out of jail, and then you would need to come back and fix this with the judge on Monday. I am sorry, but that is your only option." I said, "Now sir, why do I have to post bond for a crime I did not commit, can't you just change my plea to guilty and I will pay the $26 so I can get out of here?" "I have enough money in my belongings which they confiscated when I came to jail." All I knew was I had to get out of there. There was absolutely no way I wanted to spend any more time in jail. I had recalled that I only had $35 or $40 left that I had put in my valuable bag when they checked me in by Daytona's circus tent squad. It was enough to pay the $26 fine, even though it was admission to a crime I did not commit. I had to get out of there. The officer raised his eyebrows and calmly said, "No son, I cannot change the plea, only the judge is allowed to do that. You must post a $50 bond, and then come back on Monday and this can get all cleared up."

By now I was livid with anger, rage and fear. I knew I could not afford to post a $50 bond. What was I going to do? I told the officer that all I had was $35 or $40 and did not have $50. I think he really felt for me, but said I could keep calling my buddies and they would have to come to the jail to make up the difference. By now it was 12:30 p.m. When I got back to the cell, and asked for my phone call, they promptly escorted me to the phone. I called the hotel frantically and asked to be connected to my buddy's room. As you can probably imagine, by 12:45 p.m. on the last day of Daytona Beach, it was highly unlikely that any of my teammates would be in their room. But I had to call them. There was no way I was going to call my parents and try to explain this whole fiasco to them, much less ask for the balance to get out of jail.

The telephone rang and rang. I let it keep ringing until the jail officer said my time was up. I was allowed to keep calling like this once every hour, and continued to do so until finally between 5 and 6 p.m., someone finally answered the phone. It was my offensive center Bo whom I played next to on the offensive line. Bo, I am in jail at the city of Daytona Beach and I need you to come and pick me up! Bo started laughing hysterically. "You are in jail, are you kidding me?" They knew I was conservative and was the least likely of any of us to have been thrown in jail. Bo slipped the phone away from his mouth and started to announce it to the rest of my teammates who were in the hotel room, and I heard a chorus of wild laughter in the background. Finally I lost it, I started sobbing and emphatically told Bo, "Stop it Bo! Come to the jail and get me out of here, before I go crazy!" Bo was 6'4", 270 pounds and an All-American center and a big tough guy with a huge heart. He could tell from my voice that I was not making this story up, and he drove over and got me out as quickly as he could. It took about a half-hour or forty-five minutes for him to get there. Bo gave me the $15.00 I needed to post bond and I was finally free at last. I was never so happy to see my friends and be out of that jail cell.

I told you this story to give you insight into the last most humbling meeting I had to have. It was the meeting with my head football coach to explain why we were two days late for spring football practice. At least this meeting was a meeting in which I knew the other party, Coach Harkema. The meeting that Linda, Mollie and I were preparing for with Johnny and his parents was even more humbling because we had never met Johnny's parents much less even Johnny. The two of them had engaged in premarital sex and now our daughter was carrying his child. In the football meeting, I had to first call coach on the telephone, and then meet with him once I returned home to Grand Rapids; I had to meet with him face to face. When I called Coach Harkema on the telephone it was difficult, but the face to face meeting was even tougher. How could I as one of the leaders of my team be thrown in jail? What was he going to think of me? Would he think I was lying just to get a few more days of sun at the beach? What would my teammates think of me? It was up to that point in my life, my most humbling experience.

As it turned out, we stayed until that following Monday. I went back to the courthouse early Monday morning to speak with the judge. He would not change the charge to hitchhiking probably because there was no law against it, but more importantly to him was the fact, that the citation was written for open container in public and until a trial was set, he had to take the officer's word, not mine. I learned several important lessons from this, not the least of which was sometimes even the law enforcement system can make mistakes. I knew one thing, there was no way I ever wanted to spend another night incarcerated.

As Linda and I prepared for the meeting, we said a quick little prayer. We asked the Holy Spirit to guide our conversation and keep our emotions in check. Suddenly, there was a knock on our front door. As we came to the door, I thought, "Lord, please give me strength." The James were also very nervous as they entered our home. I forced an awkward smile and extended my hand to each of them and invited them into our home. I made sure that when I shook Johnny's hand for the first time, that I put the vice grip/bear claw squeeze on him to let him know I meant business and keep him on his toes. To my surprise, he was small and skinny in stature, but gave a very nice and firm handshake himself. After I hung up their coats, Linda invited them to sit in our living room. In all the years we have lived in our home, we have probably sat in the room less than 10 times. But it was a formal room right off our entrance and we could quickly say our peace and they could make a rapid departure, so it was really awkward in that first meeting.

I am sure if we had met the James' in any other circumstance, we would have bonded easier and quicker. The tension that we all felt was suffocating. We started out small talking; I asked Johnny's dad what he did for a living and he asked me the same. The wives remarked about the furniture and were small talking a little. Johnny appeared terrified of me and sat listless on the couch without much expression and his eyes cast downward with little if any eye contact. He was about 5' 9" tall and maybe 145 pounds with a short haircut, blond hair and blue eyes. He barely said a word the whole meeting.

Finally, I shifted the conversation to what we were all there to discuss. Mollie's pregnancy. I started it off by saying, "First of all, we realize how difficult it was for you to come over here tonight and we would like to thank you. It takes courage on your part, and Linda and I want to let you know it means a lot to us." I saw their expressions relax a little and I knew they felt a little more comfortable. I continued, "When your son and our daughter decided to have premarital, unprotected sex, THEY made a very serious error in judgment. Unfortunately, 95% of the consequences of that error are now on my daughter and our family. I am quite sure that neither of our families would have signed up to get their first grandchild this way. But the reality is Mollie is pregnant with Johnny's child, our grandchild." I knew from Mollie already that Johnny was their only child and they did not have any grandchildren. However, I later learned that this was Johnny's father's second marriage and he had a daughter from his first marriage that lived with his ex-wife. I went on to tell them as weird as it may sound to them, I was actually proud of Mollie. "We are Christians and have raised Mollie and all of our children to know HIM and the difference between right and wrong." "We have left the decision up to her and she has already made the most important decision, which is to give the baby life. Mollie believes as do we, that you should accept the consequences of your decisions. As such, she has decided to give our grandchild life. It is not the baby's fault that they made this error in judgment."

I went on to tell them further that Mollie is leaning toward keeping the baby, but is considering adoption. I asked them if they would honor and respect her decision. They said that they would. They gave us their commitment that they would support whatever Mollie's final decision was. I indicated to them that she may change her mind back and forth as time goes on, but that I would appreciate their support to support Mollie's final decision.

Up until this point in the conversation, I had done 95% of all the talking. Now it was their turn to share their point of view on the matter, and Johnny's mother took the floor. Inside, I was churning with anxiety and emotions. I was hopeful that they would let us know that they too were Christians and as such, supported giving the baby life as much as we did. Let me tell you fathers out there, that despite how much you think you are against abortion, the true litmus test of your faith on this issue is when your own teenage daughter becomes pregnant. Then and only then, will you truly know what kind of commitment you have to your faith.

We all shifted our eyes to Cathy, Johnny's mom, who was sitting Indian style on our couch next to her son. She was their chief spokesperson and you could tell from her first words that she was used to getting her way. She said that they, too, were shocked and disappointed by this news. But, they would support whatever decision Mollie made, if the child was in fact their son's child. "If!" I thought, "what do you mean if?" She went on to say it was nothing against Mollie, but they did not know her, much the same as we did not know their son Johnny. She said, "We just want to make sure." She went on further to say that they do not want to put their son's name on the birth certificate and learn later after a paternity test that their son was not the baby's father. She said she had done some "checking" and it was very difficult to get the birth certificate changed after the fact. She concluded by saying, "I hope you can appreciate and understand where we are coming from."

By now, my anxiety had turned to anger and it was about at the boiling point. After I calmed down later, I did understand where they were coming from. They did not know Mollie, but her lack of tact was not appreciated nor admired. It was a terrible first impression. She had basically accused my daughter of being some kind of tramp or slut, just 10 minutes after meeting her for the first time. As a father, I wanted to punch her husband in the mouth and tell them where to go, and throw them out of our house. Thankfully, the Holy Spirit came to my aid. He helped me "buckle my chin strap" and play the next play.

I looked at her for a long awkward moment and in the silence I could feel the Lord say, "Don't focus on her Dick, look at her son Johnny." I turned to look at Johnny. Here was an 18-year-old young man letting his mommy do his talking. What did this feel like for him? As I gazed at him, his eyes went from looking at his mom with a frown, to me and immediately down to the floor. I knew this poor kid knew that he was the father of Mollie's baby, but his mommy Cathy was used to running the show.

As his mother's only child, she was trying to protect him. However, I felt that if he was any kind of a man, he would step up, silence his mom and tell her, "Mom that is enough, Mollie is not that kind of girl. I am the father and I will take responsibility." However, Johnny's eyes remained downcast and he would not look up, nor would he stand up against his mother. This was a brilliant foreshadowing of what I would later come to learn about Johnny and his mother. She definitely called all the shots.

In any case, after the long silence, I finally said, "Well you guys do what you think you need to do." "But I have to tell you that my daughter is not a tramp. If she tells me that Johnny is the father, he is the father. She assures us that this was her first time. I do have to admit that I am surprised she put herself in this situation, but you guys do what you have to do." The whole time I said this, I was looking with dagger eyes at their son, whose eyes kept shifting from the floor to mine for a quick second and back down to the floor. After this exchange of pleasantries, we knew "the meeting" was over and we could not wait to escort them out of our home and off our premises.

Karl, Johnny's father, did ask Johnny if he wanted to say anything just prior to the meeting being adjourned. I took this as a hopeful sign. Karl seemed to have a heart and appeared to try and open the door for his son to make an admission, apology or state his own opinions. Johnny simply looked over to his dad and said, "No, I have nothing to say." With that I stood up and said, "Well, thanks a lot for taking the time to come over here. We will be in touch." Linda and I awkwardly searched for words to say, amidst our anger, hurt and pride. Pride can be a difficult thing to swallow, but it even is more difficult to swallow in a situation like this. I got their coats from our closet, shook their hands and promptly escorted them to the door. Linda exchanged phone numbers with Cathy, just prior to them leaving. "The meeting" was now done, but our association with the James family had only just begun. Hopefully things would smooth out as time went on. It was by far the most difficult meeting and humbling meeting I have ever had in my life. I remember thinking at the time of their departure from our home that based on this first meeting, I would need to "buckle my chin strap" especially with Johnny's mom. That was an understatement!

*Isaiah Chapter 11 Verse 2 & 3*
*"The Spirit of the Lord shall rest upon him; a spirit of wisdom and of understanding, a spirit of knowledge and fear of the Lord, and in his delight shall be the fear of the Lord."*

In all difficult situations in life the Lord will send his Holy Spirit to help you have wisdom and understanding. But to do that for you, you must have a relationship with Him. You must have what Isaiah calls fear which really is not fear but rather the ultimate show of confidence and respect to turn everything over to Him. In this situation of "the meeting" of three individuals I had never met, I was humbled but at the same time, Jesus sent me His Holy Spirit to give me wisdom and understanding along with guarded patience. When someone you have never met insults you, or your family or loved one, how will you react? If you buckle your chin strap with the Lord and submit to Him, He will help you with any difficulty in life no matter how large or small the task.

# Chapter 5
# 16 and Pregnant

*Isaiah Chapter 4 Verse 6*
*"for over all the Lord's glory shall be shelter and*
*protection, shade from the parching heat of day refuge*
*and cover from storm and rain."*

Once the "decision" was made and the meeting was held, it was time to shift our focus to life for Mollie as a 16-year-old and pregnant. As you can imagine, we did truly feel like we were exposed to the parching heat of day, and its storm clouds and rain seemed to fall at every fork in our journey. Thankfully, the Lord's glory did provide Mollie protection, shade and shelter from all of these storms and heat. What a wonderful Lord we have.

After we all got over the initial shock of the news and Mollie had made her decision, we tried to live our life as normal as possible. We went back to the same routines, the same rules, and the same daily activities. However, we soon learned that try as we may, the reality of being 16 and pregnant kept hitting us all smack in the face. The fact was, a baby was growing inside Mollie's womb and we needed to face this head on. Life was anything but normal for Mollie especially, no matter how normal we tried to keep it.

When I was playing football, I just had to keep practicing and working hard to put myself in a position to be successful and to win my personal battles on the gridiron. As teams in high school and college, we would go through routines, but inevitably come game time, you would have to make adjustments in order to win. No game ever went according to the script or game plan.

That is what we had to do with Mollie at 16 and being pregnant. We tried to go through routines but adjust to the things that were happening in order to put her in a position to win. Our first task that we helped Mollie with was picking an OB/GYN. We knew from our dealings with the doctor who confirmed "The News," that there was absolutely no way we wanted to use that health care system to deliver Mollie's baby. We decided to check out a few different healthcare providers in our community.

The first one we went to ended up being the one we chose. However, it was almost not even a choice. Linda and I drove to this particular clinic and spoke to the receptionist. We were somewhat embarrassed to tell the receptionist that our 16-year-old daughter was pregnant and needed to find an OB/GYN. The lady was very kind and understanding. We told her that our main requirement was that the doctor be a woman. Linda had all four of our children delivered by a male OB/GYN. We felt Mollie would be more comfortable with a woman, and when we asked her, she agreed. There was no way Mollie wanted a man delivering her baby, much less checking her female anatomy every month. We had to find a good one and an OB/GYN that preferably was a woman.

As we told the receptionist this as quietly as we could, there were several people in the waiting area listening. It felt very awkward. She proceeded to give us two possible doctors. One was a younger woman and was there in their local office, three days a week. The other one was older and she was only in their local office one day a week. If we chose this older doctor, chances were we would have to drive thirty minutes away from our community for some of the appointments. We decided to make an appointment with the younger doctor since she was only 28 and was headquartered there at their local office three days a week. Her name was Dr. Helen Morgan.

Her receptionist, however, could not make an appointment. She told us we needed to go and make the appointment with one of her schedulers. In order to do this, we needed to walk back to Dr. Morgan's clinic area which was about a hundred and fifty feet behind the receptionist desk. She told us that she would love to make the appointment, however, all appointments needed to be coordinated through Dr. Morgan's scheduler.

Linda and I were both relieved that this receptionist lady was so kind and helpful. She proceeded to call Dr. Morgan's scheduler and explain that two parents were here to make an appointment with Dr. Morgan to discuss care for their 16-year-old daughter who was pregnant. After talking a few minutes on the telephone with the scheduler, the receptionist proceeded to actually get up and walk us through the building which was quite large, but cut up like a maze. As Linda and I walked with her, hand-in-hand, we smiled and felt as though God was helping us find the right doctor for our daughter. It was a big relief.

As we approached the scheduler's office, the receptionist turned and said, "Just take a right at the next corner, walk through the door, and Dr. Morgan's scheduler will be on your right at the window." We thanked the lady for her assistance and headed through the door to make the appointment. I thought to myself in silent prayer, "Thank you Lord for guiding our steps." We proceeded to walk through the door when "POW!" we were hit with another punch to the abdomen. The scheduler happened to be one of Mollie's best friend's mother. Linda had led the way through the door as I held it, and as soon as she saw Barb, she turned to me with a look of horror on her face. She was floored and did not want to let Barb know that our Mollie had been the 16-year-old that the receptionist had spoken to her about. Luckily, Barb had not seen Linda though since she was facing to the side looking on her computer screen. Linda made a quick 180° turn to come back through the doorway. She whispered, "Come on Dick, we're out of here!"

Confused, I had proceeded through the door and by then, Barb had turned around and could see me. Before I could make the same 180 degree turn and leave, Barb said, "Well, hi Dick, what brings you here?" I knew from my selling career to answer a question with a question when you need time to think so I said, "Hi Barb, I did not know you worked here. How long have you worked here?" By changing the question directed to me back to her, I could think for a moment. We small talked for a little bit and then I told her a little white lie. I casually said that I was actually lost and that I was looking for the x-ray department. "Can you tell me where it is?" She had not seen Linda, so it was not as awkward as it felt. She directed me to the x-ray department. After exchanging a few more catch-up conversations about her daughter Ashley, her new house and twins, I made a beeline out of there. By now, Linda was sobbing and had headed for our car parked outside.

As I walked back to the car, the Holy Spirit told me, "Dick, there is a reason I have directed you here. Barb knows Linda, you, Mollie and your family. She will help you with Dr. Morgan. Trust in Me." I had coached Barb's daughter Ashley in soccer for two or three years and Mollie and Ashley were close friends. When I opened the car door, Linda was having a major meltdown, sobbing uncontrollably and repeating over and over, "Why is this happening?" We sat in the car for a good 10 minutes or so until I eventually got her calmed down. I told her that the Holy Spirit was guiding us there and this was a sign from Him that this was the correct choice for Mollie's doctor. After all, Barb knew Mollie and us. With Mollie still being in high school, she would give her preferential treatment in scheduling appointments, and helping us with communications, etc. to the doctor.

Linda was worried that once Barb knew, she would tell Ashley and soon the rumor mill would be ramping up with stories about Mollie and her being pregnant. I really did not care about the rumor mill, or the fact that others would find out, as I knew eventually this would happen anyway. However, I had to be cognizant of Linda's feelings and show her that I understood where she was coming from. It was the first of many episodes I experienced with Linda like this, as we experienced the journey through a teenage daughter's pregnancy. Women think and respond differently to things and each time that these philosophical reactions happened, I had to "buckle my chin strap" and play the next play. This was especially hard for me to do. I sometimes could not understand what planet Linda's feelings were coming from, but I had to try my best to be understanding, patient and sympathetic. I proceeded to comfort Linda as best I could. I told her I understood her feelings, even though philosophically, I disagreed.

I began asking her a few questions. Do you think we will be able to keep this a secret? Won't Barb find out eventually anyway? Can we really stop the rumor mill? I knew the answers to these questions and so did Linda, even though it was difficult to face them. Finally after discussing this in the car for ten or fifteen minutes, Linda and I agreed and said a quick prayer.

"Let's go back inside and make the appointment," she finally said and that is how we met Dr. Helen Morgan.

Dr. Helen Morgan was a young 28-year-old doctor who looked as if she herself had just graduated from high school. She was about 5'7" tall with shoulder length jet black hair, kind big brown eyes and soft yellow skin of Asian descent. When we first met Dr. Morgan, we had no idea that she was six months pregnant with her first child. This too, was actually too good to be true! Not only was she only 12 years older than Mollie and a woman, but she was walking the same journey that our Mollie was as a first-time mother-to-be. She was only about four months ahead of Mollie. She would be able to really relate well with what Mollie was feeling and going through as she herself was only months ahead of Mollie. We again thanked God for this blessing.

Dr. Morgan put Mollie on prenatal vitamins and scheduled her monthly exams for the next three months. When Mollie had these appointments with Dr. Morgan, she would always be more relaxed and confident in the changes her body was going through. However, after being on the vitamins for almost a week we experienced another blow to the midsection. Mollie started getting morning sickness every morning. This was especially hard to watch and listen to, for both Linda and me. Why did this have to happen? Linda had all four of our children and had never experienced even one day of morning sickness. "Why was God doing this to Mollie?" Linda would mutter, "I never had this happen to me!" I would tell her repeatedly throughout Mollie's pregnancy that just because your body reacted that way, does not mean this is how Mollie's will react. "Everyone's body is different and remember that Mollie is only 16, you were nine years older when you had your first pregnancy." I had to force her to recall the events and just how fortunate she had been not ever having experienced morning sickness, headaches, and constant drowsiness.

We called Dr. Morgan after these morning sickness episodes happened for four or five days in a row. They happened both at home and in school and started to affect Mollie's desire to attend school. We thought she could be allergic to the vitamins or maybe Dr. Morgan could switch to a different type of prenatal vitamins. When Dr. Morgan finally called us back, she said to take the vitamins at dinner time instead of at breakfast. So we switched and it did help Mollie. She still had morning sickness and nausea symptoms, but only once every two or three days. These bouts with "Morning Sickness" continued for the first four months of Mollie's pregnancy. When they finally stopped, it was a welcome sigh of relief. Believe me as a father, you do not enjoy seeing your baby girl endure this every morning at 6:00 a.m., as she got ready to go to school. It literally tore my guts out to see her vomit and then not be able to eat breakfast every morning because she was so nauseous.

School was a blessing and a curse for Mollie. How could a 16-year old pregnant girl walk the halls among other students who would often snicker, jeer and point their fingers at Mollie? Mollie attended a local high school that actually consisted of three high schools on a half square mile plot of land. The schools were set up on a campus park theme in order to share resources, facilities and staff to educate over 6000 children on site. They had approximately 2000 students at each high school. The students attend classes in all three buildings during their four years of school. They are allowed 10 minutes to walk between buildings, which during the winter in the snow, rain and wind, can be quite a task. Each high school has separate sports teams, but they have a combined marching band and a combined yearbook. The yearbook is about three inches thick.

As you can probably imagine, the start of the school year was somewhat challenging for Mollie. By now, most of the people in her friendship circle knew that she was pregnant and had decided to keep the baby. The rumor mill was in full production throughout August and September. Many students whom Mollie did not even know would come up and ask her bluntly, "Was she pregnant?" Others would write things in their FaceBook or MySpace accounts about her. To Mollie's credit, she never once complained about this gossip and badgering nor the subsequent stares and whispering that occurred as she walked the halls alone.

Yes, she did walk the halls alone. The father of the baby, Johnny James (JJ) had decided to deny that he was the father thanks to his mother's paternity test desires. He decided to acquire another girlfriend and basically ignore Mollie for most of the pregnancy. They actually had one class together and he acted as if she was not even in the classroom. Mollie was hurt by this, obviously, but she got through it thanks to support from her friends and family.

As the school year progressed, JJ's friends actually spread rumors that Mollie had caused JJ's breakup with his new girlfriend. When his new girlfriend learned a few months into their relationship that JJ had gotten Mollie pregnant, she immediately called it off. Can you believe that? With all Mollie was going through, not only did he abandon her, but now he had told his friends that Mollie had caused this breakup with his new girlfriend. This infuriated me. I wanted to take him and his father in my backyard and have my son and I teach them a lesson. However, thankfully this never happened.

the news had spread that Mollie was pregnant, came old news and was basically treated as any student that walked the halls in a 6000 plus student high school. Most of the other students did not even know her. With the baggy clothes that the kids today wear, many of her fellow students could not even notice that she was pregnant. I was thankful for this. If she had attended a small rural school with 200 to 300 students, everyone would know who she was and her condition. The pressure on her would have been enormous. Thankfully in this large school district with so many students, she would just blend in and be considered one in the pack.

The one thing that I found truly remarkable about the high schools were the staff all the way from the superintendent to the counselor and to the teachers. None of them were judgmental. None of them were arrogant or flippant about Mollie's pregnancy. Many of them went above and beyond the protocols and rules to help Mollie and make her journey as easy as possible. The first person we contacted prior to classes beginning in her 11th grade summer was the counseling office. We were assigned a new counselor who had transferred from another school district; her name was Mrs. Michelle Brunch. Mrs. Brunch was a woman in her late forties with short brown hair, a round happy face and bright blue eyes. Once we got to know her, it turned out that she was a sister-in-law to one of the teachers my wife Linda taught with at Tonda Elementary School in our community. This, too, I believe was not a coincidence. It seemed everywhere we turned, the Lord put people in positions to help Mollie and our family who were connected to our circle of friends.

What an amazing blessing Mrs. Brunch was to Mollie and our family. She helped us with all the decisions Mollie had to make regarding school and classes. She told Mollie of two alternative education programs and facilities she could attend which were run by the county. She informed us that Mollie would even be allowed to bring her baby to either of these alternative education centers after it was born while she completed her high school education. If Mollie decided to transfer to one of these alternative education schools, they had daycare centers at each location which would help her with her baby. She also explained that Mollie could continue to attend high school at the park if she desired. She explained that technically a pregnancy is not a disability or an injury so she would not be able to receive in-home service and support. Therefore, if she chose to stay up at the high schools located in the Educational Park, she would need to continue to go to class as close up to the delivery of the baby as possible. She told us of the United Way run teenage pregnancy counseling service that Mollie could attend for no charge in order to talk with others who have or were journeying down the same path of teenage pregnancy. We actually did check this service out and Mollie utilized this regularly once every other week to help her deal with things such as goal setting, planning for the baby, learning about the pregnancy and the delivery, etc. Mrs. Brunch also made repeated efforts to put Mollie with teachers who would be understanding and helpful to Mollie. She limited Mollie's walks between the buildings to once a day. She treated Mollie like she was her own daughter and helped her through her entire junior year as a pregnant teen. She was phenomenal!

Many of Mollie's teachers were unbelievably kind and supportive to her. I actually had one teacher breakdown and cry as I told him of Mollie's pregnancy. I decided to attend parents' night during the first week of school. Parents' night is a night which starts at 7:00 p.m.. Basically, you become your daughter or son and you travel between all the buildings and classrooms mirroring the journey that your child takes each day of class. The teachers introduce themselves to you and explain their expectations along with distributing their contact information so you can call or e-mail them with any concerns throughout the year. Each teacher gets 10 minutes to speak to the parents and then the bell rings. Once the bell rings, the parents move from the first through seventh period of their child's day and are allowed the 10 minutes travel time between classes just as their child is allowed. It was a great way to get a feel for what your child's day was like with their teachers and the traveling between three high schools all located on a half mile square until the day's simulation of your child's classes was done. Linda and I were familiar with the drill as we had attended parents' night with our older children who had previously attended the high schools in the Educational Park. This did give the parents an appreciation of just how difficult it can sometimes be walking a third of a mile between buildings and trying to find the right classrooms. It also gave the parents a feel for just how crowded the Educational Park can get with people in the hallways, on the sidewalks and in the classrooms.

In any event, I had decided to attend parents' night and introduce myself to each of Mollie's teachers. At the completion of their speeches, I pulled every single teacher aside and made sure that I waited until no other parents were in earshot. I waited until all other parents had left the room and I would go on to tell each teacher that my daughter was 16 and pregnant. I told them that Mollie would need their understanding and help and that she was a Christian and did not believe in murdering innocent children. As such, she would be giving her baby the ultimate gift of life.

In one of these introductions to a teacher, I had to wait for at least three other parents to finish talking to the teacher. He was a very nice young man and about 32 years of age. Prior to my speaking to him, each of the other parents were boasting about their son or daughter on how smart they were and how they had gotten straight A's so far in high school and boast further that their son/daughter would work hard to ace his class, etc., etc. By the time it was my turn to talk, I think he had been peppered enough with parents bragging and I actually shocked him. I told him that my daughter was not a straight "A" student but rather a student who had struggled to get good grades so far in high school. I told him that she was a good kid though with a meek and tender heart. I told him that we had just learned she was pregnant and at 16 it was very tough on her. I went on to tell him that we were Christians, and as such, that we did not believe in murdering innocent children. I told him that she was going to live with the consequences and take responsibility for her decision. He was floored. He got tears in his eyes and said that he was a Christian, too, and would do his best to help Mollie. Each teacher I told this story to was very kind, understanding and very willing to help. Each teacher was given my e-mail address and I asked them to feel free to email me regularly on how they thought she was doing. I would periodically e-mail them on Mollie's progress in their class and her challenges or progress with the pregnancy. I had been very skeptical of the Plymouth Canton Educational Park (PCEP) up until this time, but I learned that most of the teachers really do care about kids.

The only negative thing that happened at PCEP, was a slip and fall accident. When Mollie was approximately six months pregnant, she slipped and fell on the ice on the sidewalk one day while walking between the schools. We live approximately one mile from the school, so I would give Mollie a ride each day to school. One morning it was minus 10° outside air temperature and all the other schools in the county that day had closed due to the temperature with the exception of our district and one other school district. I could not believe it as a parent that our children would have to attend school on this particular day. Especially since they are the only district in the state of Michigan who have a campus of buildings where you have to walk outside between all these high schools approximately a third of a mile apart. Mollie begged me to stay home that morning, but I made her go. However, as I dropped her off that particular morning, I noticed that the sidewalk was still dusted with snow and not salted. I told Mollie to be careful walking and she gave me her usual snide reply, "Yeah Dad, don't worry." Well, my worries this time had blossomed into a slip and fall and luckily nothing happened to the baby since she caught herself.

I was extremely disappointed and wrote an e-mail to the superintendent of schools after repeated phone calls getting a busy signal at the high school principal's office. The superintendent had gotten over 500 e-mails and several hundred phone calls from perturbed parents that day for deciding to have school on this particular day. He answered my e-mail at about 10:30 p.m. that night as I had been one of the last to write him. In my email to him, I was careful not to complain about his decision to have school that day. I told him that having class was his decision to make. I did, however, tell him of Mollie's slip and fall at the high school and that she was six months pregnant. I told him that I personally had observed a light dusting of snow that morning when I dropped her off at school and that as a parent I expected that if he holds school, that the walkways should be safe. He told me first he was sorry and would check into why the walks had not been salted, he told me his rationale as to why he decided to have school that day. He also said although he was not supposed to say this, that he will pray that God blesses our daughter. This was said by the leader of a public school district. I was especially pleased to know that the leader of our school district was a Christian man and believed in God. I told him so in my reply e-mail and wished him also God's blessings.

As Mollie journeyed through the school year we were amazed at her academic progress. The progress on the report card showed excellent results with 3.1 and 3.3 GPA's. Prior to her junior year, Mollie had struggled and was barely a 2.0 GPA student. It seemed that being pregnant did have an upside to it. It forced Mollie to focus on what was really important in life. Education, work and planning were the three areas she really improved in. She now had a reason and a motivation to be more serious about applying herself to her studies. Her baby was going to need a mom who could support him or her and without education, you don't succeed in life.

She also decided on her own to get a job. There were too many nights I would come home from work and be forced to listen to my wife complain about how tired Mollie always was. How she would come home and sleep right after school. On days before Mollie had to go to work on the weekends, she would sleep in very late until noon or even 1:00 p.m. She was always very tired throughout the whole pregnancy. Linda could not understand this. She had worked right up until delivery of all four of our children. She kept a tidy home, worked, made dinner and paid the bills without ever being tired. Why was Mollie always so tired? She was never this tired when she was pregnant with our children. My wife Linda is a go-getter and is constantly on the move. I once again had to remind her that all pregnancies are different and that all women handle them differently. Linda definitely was worried about her little girl and she needed a punching bag to vent her frustrations on. I had to be that punching bag. I knew that I had been hit much harder than this both on the gridiron and in life, and I understood my role was to be this punching bag for her. I buckled my chin strap and endured the next play.

The job Mollie acquired was at Jimmy John's restaurant which is a fast food chain that makes sub sandwiches. Later she would add a second job so she was working four to five days a week to earn money to pay baby expenses, attending school and getting good grades. Linda and I were both relieved and thankful for this. We were also very proud of Mollie as she did this all on her own initiative. I had been especially determined that we would not make it easy on Mollie. My other children each had received a car from my wife and me, although it was a used one to drive in their junior and senior year of high school. We decided not to buy Mollie a car since her car was the baby growing in her womb. We could not reward or make it easy on her. We both knew that for the rest of her life, it was going to be a difficult road. However, I was very happy for Mollie. She never once complained about not having a car either.

At about six months along, Dr. Morgan decided to order an ultrasound to see the progress of the baby's growth. Mollie and Linda had been hearing the baby's heartbeat at the monthly checkups, but now they would finally get the opportunity to see what our grandchild looked like in an ultrasound. It was truly a remarkable experience. The technology of ultrasounds today was far more advanced from 20 years earlier when we had ultrasounds for our children. You could see every smallest detail. You could see the baby's organs, it's heart, lungs, kidneys, bones, eyes, ears, fingers, toes, and, yes, you could easily tell if it was a

boy or girl. Linda and I were old-school traditi
and elected never to find out what sex our cl
were when we had our children's ultrasounds.
however, lives in the new school 21st-century
wanted to know the sex. Let me just say that when the
ultrasound technician maneuvered the sound
instrument between the babies legs you knew in an
instant that he was a boy. He was well endowed like
his grandpa... With tears in our eyes we all held hands
throughout the ultrasound and gave thanks to God for
Mollie's son who appeared healthy and growing
according to schedule.

Now that Mollie knew she was going to have a son, she
told everyone. So the news spread to JJ and suddenly
he started to come around a little more often. His new
girlfriend had broken up with him when she heard
that he had gotten Mollie pregnant. Although he and
his parents were not sure that the baby was his as of
yet, they suddenly and inexplicably became very
interested. My wife Linda wondered if the ultrasound
had showed it was a girl what their reaction would
have been. She seriously doubted that JJ would have
been as interested, much less his parents, who
wanted to pass on their last name, had the test
revealed the baby was a girl. In any case, Mollie was
truly starting to get excited. She now knew that she
was having a son. She could start planning for his
room redecoration, his clothes, his name and the baby
showers. Baby showers? Who was going to give a
pregnant teenager a baby shower? Wouldn't that be
rewarding the teen for having premarital sex?
Wouldn't we be sending a mixed signal to other
teenage girls and Mollie's friends? Linda was having a
major problem with this, too. She did not want other
people to think we were rewarding our daughter for
becoming pregnant as a teenager out of wedlock. She
also did not want to send this message to Mollie's

friends. "Go ahead and have sex with boys. Get pregnant and we will throw you a baby shower!"

I understood her perspective here, however, a baby is a gift from God no matter how he or she arrives. After much prayer, thought and discussion with friends, Linda and I agreed to give Mollie a baby shower. It turned out that she actually had three baby showers. One shower was with her high school friends and their moms in her friend Samantha's home. One was with all the teachers my wife Linda worked with at Tonda Elementary School and one with our family relatives in my brother's home. Each of these showers it turned out was a blessing for both Mollie and Linda. It taught Mollie the value of friends and relationships in sharing the joy of childbirth. It also taught Linda that she needed her friends too, and that none of them judged her or Mollie for her transgression of premarital sex. I was more and more thankful after each baby shower to see my wife's worry turn to joy and anxious enthusiasm at the coming of a blessed child. Women need these showers to commiserate and share in the excitement.

Once the showers were over, we had to set up the room in boy colors. The bedroom directly across the hall from Mollie's bedroom in our house was empty as our oldest daughter Amber had graduated from college and was a teacher at an elementary school in Orlando, Florida. We decided to retrofit her room as it was also the closest bedroom to Mollie's bedroom. Amber's bedroom had been painted a deep purple color and there was no way that Mollie wanted her son to be in a purple room. Linda is a very talented painter and got right into helping Mollie pick the color scheme and the two of them worked together to paint the room blue, green and white. Once the room was repainted, we had to pick up a crib, a changing table and rocking chair. All of these activities served as medicine to heal the wounded souls. It kept the girls busy and their minds off the worries of the baby's delivery, the feedings, the late nights, the court battles, and the child nurturing which would all come soon.

Being 16 and pregnant is not an easy journey. It is not easy for the teenage girl nor is it easy for her mother. It certainly can put a strain on your marriage as well. But thankfully through God's mercy and grace, you can endure and overcome. You can help lead your daughter and your family through this storm. The Lord can be your shelter from the storm if you let Him. The mercy that He extended to Mollie and our family through Mollie's journey can be extended to any family whose teenage daughter is pregnant. You simply need to look for the Lord walking on the water as Jesus did, and He will calm the storm as He did with His disciples in the Sea of Galilee. The Lord is there with you in the people you reach out to and the ones He sends along the journey. Have faith in this journey and remember that as in football: expect to get knocked down and your helmet smashed off once in awhile. It comes with the territory and is really part of the game. But as in a football game, you need to get back up Buckle Your Chin Strap and keep playing the game.

*John Chapter 6 Verse 18 & 19*
*"The sea was stirred up because a strong wind was blowing when they had rowed about three or four miles, they saw Jesus walking on the sea and coming to the boat, and they began to be afraid."*

In our daughter's teenage pregnancy journey, the rough sea and wind blowing was a difficult waterway to navigate. The boat we were in represented our family, friends and the church. We saw Jesus walking and coming near the boat repeatedly through the journey. Jesus was repeatedly represented by our friends who helped us, the teachers and counselors who were merciful to Mollie, and the healthcare providers that He led us to. It was indeed a journey of faith and one in which we too, like the disciples, had to row extremely hard for three or four miles in rough and hard-to-navigate waters. The Sea of Galilee is actually about 12 miles long by seven miles wide. It is a very deep waterway with hills surrounding it. If you are thrown overboard in these seas when the wind blows, you must be a strong swimmer as most people would drown and perish. None of us wanted Mollie to drown. We were terrified that the pregnancy would kill our daughter's life; Life as we had hoped and dreamed for her. We did not want her to drown. We learned through the journey that the Lord wants you to understand that you and your daughter must be willing to put forth the effort to row your boat for a good portion of the journey, "three or four miles," or more perhaps. But He will send His mercy to each of you to calm the waters so your boat can arrive on shore safely. Each of you will no longer have to be afraid. Whether you have to row the boat three, four or even seven miles the width or twelve miles the entire length of the journey, the sea will be rough. If you try to do it alone, you may fall out of the boat, perish, drown or simply stay lost at sea. But if you and your daughter put your faith in Jesus, search for Him walking towards you each step of the journey, your journey will be safe and you will reach dry land. We did and you can, too.

# Chapter 6
## Miracle of Life

*Genesis Chapter 2 Verse 7*
*"The Lord God formed man out of the clay of the*
*ground and blew into his nostrils the breath of life and*
*so man became a living being."*

Have you ever seen a miracle? I have been graced by God to have witnessed five in my lifetime with the births of my four children and now my first grandchild. It is truly an amazing event to participate in. When a newborn infant comes into the world, new life abounds and all the troubles of life seem to stand still, in a frozen perfect moment. As you focus on God's gift and miracle now out of the mother's womb, you realize that you have just witnessed a miracle. What was life going to be like for this little miracle? Will he or she be happy? How will he or she change my life? What talents has God blessed him or her with? What will he or she accomplish in their lifetime? What is God's plan for this child? Many of these questions race through your mind as you gaze into the miracle of life of a newborn child. That is only part of the miracle you experience in the birth of a child. The rest of the miracle is experienced each day of the child's life as he breathes the breath of life put into him by our heavenly Father and Creator.

On April 18, 2007, at 8:47 p.m. after 52 hours of labor, Brayden Michael Williams was born to our daughter Mollie. It truly was a miracle, but a miracle that came with much physical and emotional pain for both my daughter Mollie and our entire family. It all began three days before on April 16.

Mollie had not been sleeping too well at night and she had gotten rather big with the growth of her child in her womb. It was a Tuesday night when Mollie laid in bed tossing and turning with discomfort and pain in her lower back. She endured that Tuesday evening and never even complained to either Linda or me. When it came time for me to wake her up, I learned that she was wide awake and had not slept much Tuesday night. It had been my practice of waking Mollie every morning at 6:00 a.m. to get ready for school. I usually rise between 5:00 a.m. and 5:30 a.m. every day. I read the daily Bible readings on the computer and write my prayers in my daily prayer journal. Here is an excerpt of what I wrote, early that Tuesday morning just prior to waking Mollie up. "Lord Jesus, bless my dear daughter Mollie and her pregnancy. I beg you Lord to help her in her labor and delivery. Please send her your Holy Spirit to help strengthen her. Please protect her and her son. Lord guide them both with your angels. Father God, open up her womb and her pelvis wide so that Brayden can slide easily out. Father help her. Lord reward her life with happiness for having chose life for her son." From this excerpt, you can see that I was very concerned. My wife Linda had struggled long and hard for over 70 hours in the birth of our first child Amber. We did not know it at the time with Linda, but her pelvis was too small to push the baby out and all of our subsequent children had to be born by cesarean section. I did not want Mollie at 16 years of age to be going through this type of trauma. Nor did I want her to have the large scar that the C-section leaves along with the skin sagging. I prayed earnestly the entire pregnancy for God's deliverance for her.

As I opened Mollie's door that April 16th morning, I turned on her light and saw that she was already sitting propped up in bed with pillows placed strategically around her back all the way up to her head. I told her it was time to get up and get ready for school. She said, "Dad, I don't think I hardly even slept last night." I asked her, "Why haven't you slept, are you nervous about the labor and delivery?" She explained, "No Dad, but my back really hurts!" "Where does your back hurt?" I asked. Mollie proceeded to show me and point to her lower back between her tailbone and waistline. Then I asked her if there was a constant pain or whether it comes and goes. She said, "It comes and goes, but only every 15 or 20 minutes." I decided to go wake my wife Linda and asked her opinion. Linda did not think it was labor, and thought it may have been from Mollie's working the night before and standing on her feet for such a long time. At the time, neither Linda nor I knew what a back labor was, nor had we even considered it a possibility for Mollie. Linda nor any of her friends or any of my sisters for that matter, had ever experienced back labor before.

So we had no clue that Mollie had in fact been in back labor all night. Linda and I decided to send Mollie to school. We told her that she had to get up and get ready for school. We knew she would miss school after the baby was born, so we were determined to minimize the number of days she missed before the baby was born. I knew that Mollie was not happy about that directive, but she just smiled and did as we asked and did not utter one word of complaint. This was a common theme throughout Mollie's entire pregnancy, labor and delivery, and life after Brayden was born. It is the one that I am most proud and thankful for. She never whined, complained or cried woe is me. I think that is one of her personal strengths that God has blessed her with. Her attitude was phenomenal for a 16 year old pregnant teen.

Mollie went to school and endured the entire day. When she got home after school that day, she was still having back pain come and go every 15 to 20 minutes. Linda decided to take Mollie to the doctor's office when she got home from teaching later that afternoon. Once she got there, Dr. Morgan checked Mollie over and discovered that she was dilated to three centimeters. She went on to tell Linda and Mollie that she was experiencing back labor contractions. Now we knew why she had been having the lower back pain. She indicated further that back labor pain was the most painful labor pains that a woman can experience and that Mollie should go home and rest. She advised Mollie that once the contractions get eight minutes apart to call the hospital. Dr. Morgan closed the conversation by telling them that she was off the next day on Thursday since that was her day off. However, she assured Mollie that she would do everything she could to try to come and deliver the baby if she happened to have it on that Thursday.

Mollie and Linda drove home from the doctor's office with a high degree of anxiety, but yet they had peace knowing that she was in labor and that Dr. Morgan would be there to deliver the baby. When she got home, Mollie laid down until dinner for about an hour. When it came time to sit down at the dinner table, she would not eat any dinner and tried to go to bed early that night around 8:00 p.m. As she went to bed, Linda and I felt terrible for having made her attend school all day while she was in back labor. We were thankful that she did not complain or worse yet go into full labor while at school.

Later that night, after two or three hours of tossing and turning in bed, she came into our bedroom around 11:00 p.m. and said that she was having back pain come and go quicker, every 10 minutes or so. Linda immediately jumped out of bed and bless her heart, took Mollie by the hand back into her bedroom. Mollie's bed was a large queen size bed, so Linda decided to get in bed with her for the rest of the night. I watched this act of love with great admiration and pride. Linda knew better than I, what was really going to happen and what Mollie was going through. She had asked earlier that day at the doctor appointment when describing the back pain to Doctor Morgan's nurse, and the nurse had told her that she was probably going to have back labor throughout the entire labor and delivery. She again reminded Linda that back labor was one of the most painful types of labor pain and Linda felt very concerned for Mollie. Linda felt guilty as did I, for sending Mollie to school that day.  Dr. Morgan had said to monitor how far apart the pains were and how long they lasted. When they got eight minutes apart or less, our orders were to call the hospital. Once we made the call to the hospital, Dr. Morgan told us that the hospital would try to get in touch with her even if it was on her day off. She had left instructions at the hospital labor and delivery floor that she wanted to be contacted regardless of the circumstances. It was her first delivery of an unwed teenage mother and she had formed a special connection and bond with Mollie.

Linda spent most of that Wednesday evening in bed with Mollie whispering, laughing and timing the back contractions. Thank God for Linda. She helped calm Mollie during this difficult time. At about 4:00 a.m., Linda came back into our bedroom and notified me that the back contractions were now eight minutes apart and that she was going to call the hospital. I had not slept either. I was nervous and anxious for Mollie as well, and could overhear the laughter, anxious giggles and the quiet whispering in the other room. The hospital staff advised us to have Mollie take a shower and then drive her to the hospital. Linda and I already had her bags packed and with an adrenaline rush, we quickly packed it in my car and waited downstairs for Mollie to finish her shower.  We decided to make a fresh pot of coffee while we waited. As we sipped on a hot black coffee we pondered what we would be experiencing the remainder of that day. We sipped our coffee together and just looked into each others eyes searching for solace and strength.

As we sat together at our kitchen table waiting for Mollie, my mind drifted off again to those days on the gridiron. I was thinking that the feeling I had was the same type of feeling I would have on the nights before our games. I thought of all the games I had played in college and in high school when we were up against a superior opponent that we were never supposed to compete with, much less win. It seemed like Mollie was up against a tough opponent too, and unfortunately, now I was a coach and could not be one of the players.

One such opponent I thought of was during my sophomore year at Grand Valley State. We were playing Northern Michigan University (NMU), the defending NCAA Division II National Champions. Although we were 8-2 for the year, we were heavy underdogs. NMU had been number one in the country all year long and was 10-0 overall. We were 40 point underdogs despite winning our conference and having given them a good game the prior year at their place, one which we should have won. This year, they had returned 20 of 22 starters that had won the National Championship the year before. They had beaten Central, Western and Eastern Michigan University's all NCAA Division I schools and their closest game of the season was a three touchdown margin. The week before they played us, they had beaten the University of Nebraska-Omaha 86 -- 0. All the newspapers and experts predicted another NMU blowout.

The night before that game, I had prayed fervently to the Lord and to St. Jude the patron saint of despair and lost hope. I decided to tape a St. Jude holy card to the sock of my right leg. On the back of the card the prayer of St. Jude reads as follows: "Most holy apostle, St. Jude, faithful servant and friend of Jesus, the Church honors and invokes you universally, as the patron of hopeless cases, of things almost despaired of. Pray for me, I am so helpless and alone. Make use I implore you, of that particular privilege given to you, to bring visible and speedy help where help is almost despaired of. Come to my assistance in this great need that I may receive the consolation and help of heaven in all my necessities, tribulations, and sufferings, particularly (here make your request) and that I may praise God with you and all the elect forever.

I promise, O blessed saint Jude to be ever mindful of this great favor, to always honor you as my special and powerful patron, and to gratefully encourage devotion to you. Amen"

My mother Janet Fern Williams, God rest her soul, was an avid believer in the power of prayer to St. Jude. She even named her last child, my sister Judy after St. Jude. She had given me the St. Jude holy card when I left for college and I had hung onto it placing it in my bible. I still have it today in my wallet!

None of the newspaper experts knew that secretly, our head coach Jim Harkema and his staff, had spent the last 10 minutes of every practice that year, preparing and working on various game plan strategies, plays, formations, coverages and defenses to beat Northern Michigan. The previous year, my freshman year, we had traveled nine hours in a bus to Marquette, Michigan, in Michigan's Upper Peninsula home of NMU only to lose our last game that year. We lost to them by a score of 21 -- 17 on a trick play that was actually illegal. They ran a play called the "Lonesome End Play" in the fourth quarter to score a come from behind victory 21 – 17. They went on to win the 1975 NCAA Division II National Championship. The play was illegal by rule, however, there was nothing we could do about it, but prepare for our revenge the following year. Our entire team felt cheated in 1975 and we were determined to let justice prevail. We knew that the next year when they would have to travel to our house on a nine hour bus ride to Allendale, Michigan, that we would be ready because we had practiced 10 minutes of every practice that year preparing to beat them.

During the rematch game with NMU, about halfway through the fourth quarter we were ahead 24 -- 14, but you could feel the momentum was swinging. In the first half we had scored 21 unanswered points. Our offense could not be stopped and our defense had executed the perfect techniques to disguise coverages and confuse their All-American quarterback Steve Mariucci. We went into the locker room at halftime sky high up 21 -- zero. In the third quarter we took the opening kickoff down inside the 30 yard line where we were stopped. We kicked a field goal and were up 24 -- zero. However, since the opening drive of the second half, our offense had sputtered partially due to our mistakes, but mostly due to Northern's defense and the adjustments they made. We had been unable to move the ball, and their offense had scored on their last two possessions to make it a 24 -- 14 score. It seemed the momentum was swinging to Northern Michigan when I went to the line of scrimmage on a third and short play. As I got to the line, suddenly three NMU players were laughing and taunting me as they pointed at St. Jude's picture which was taped to my right leg. One of them started making fun of it and me saying, "Who is that your girlfriend? Are you some kind of lover boy you blankety blank?" I told them it was not my girlfriend, that it was St. Jude my favorite patron saint. They started laughing even harder and exclaimed, "Oh, you're one of those religious freaks or something." The referee was spotting the ball and I just ignored them, gritted my teeth and silently called on St. Jude to let me blast this guy and shut his trap. Well I did manage to blast the guy on the next play, but unfortunately we did not get a first down. Before I knew it, we were in punt formation, punting the ball back to them. After making the tackle on a few yards of return at the 25 yard line, Northern Michigan's offense took over.

They promptly moved the ball decisively and methodically directly down the field inside our 20 yard line on passes that seemed to float play after play into the hands of their receivers. In only a little over two minutes they had moved the ball into scoring range and it appeared we would soon be clinging to a three-point lead. The stadium was on edge and quiet. My teammates on the sideline with me were noticeably concerned. That's when St. Jude intervened on the wings of Danny Jackson our outside linebacker I had told you about earlier in this book. Mariucci, their quarterback, dropped back to throw a quick out pattern to his fellow All-American wide receiver a guy named Maurice Mitchell, when suddenly Danny jumped the route and returned the ball 94 yards for a Grand Valley State touchdown. The stadium went wild. My teammates and I stormed the field and we jam piled on top of Danny in the end zone. We knew that this was the last and decisive blow to win the game and were thrilled to get the 15 yard penalty for excessive celebration and unsportsmanlike conduct. I don't think our coach was happy, but it was an emotion that I only experienced a few times in my life: at this game, completing the Detroit Free Press marathon with my brother David and when each of my children were born. It was euphoric!

We went on to win the game 31 -- 14 that day. Many of my teammates credited Danny's big play for winning that game. I learned something very important that day. I learned that faith is a very powerful tool when channeled through the Lord's servants. I knew that St. Jude had intervened to help Danny jump the route and I cannot help but wonder all these years since, if those three NMU guys laughing at St. Jude are still laughing. Hopefully they are not. I also learned that sometimes if you trust in God when you are not in control, He can intervene and change the suspected outcome. If you buckle your chin strap with the Lord, He will help you overcome any obstacle.

As I sipped the last few sips of coffee that April 18, 2007 morning, I felt much as I did on the sideline of that game my sophomore season at Grand Valley against NMU. I knew I had done all I could to this point to help my teenage daughter and her mother, but now the play was not in my hands. I was merely a spectator and a coach. I wanted to help my daughter but I could not deliver the baby myself. I needed the Lord to help. I needed the Holy Spirit and St. Jude to help Mollie and her son Brayden come through this labor and delivery healthy with minimal pain and/or complications. Finally, Mollie came downstairs and we were ready to pile into my truck and drive to the hospital.

It seemed that in no time, we were on our way to the hospital which was only 20 minutes or so away from our home. As we drove to the hospital, I wondered how long it would be before Mollie would deliver and if it would be on that day, April 18. I had hoped that it would not be on the 18th for quite some time. The 18th of April happened to be Mollie's birthday and I wanted her and Brayden to each have their own special day. As it turned out, they now share the same birthday, April 18. I told Mollie afterwards that when she screws up, she really picked the way to screw it up good. She did not understand what I was referring to, when I made this comment and laughed halfheartedly. I explained my point further, and told her that the one day for the rest of her life that she could be number one was on April 18. However, now even on her birthday, she will forever be number two because it will now be Brayden's birthday more than it will be hers. Brayden will be number one even on her birthday as he will be 365 days a year for the rest of her life. She laughed, but I don't think she totally understood what I meant by that reference. Someday hopefully she will.

We arrived at the hospital shortly after 6:00 a.m. It seemed quiet, but we learned later that the labor and delivery floor was actually packed to the maximum level. They even had to send patients to other floors as it was very crowded. The triage nurses checked Mollie's dilation and hooked her up on a contraction monitoring system. They reported that she had dilated to just over 5 cm and that her contractions were now just under six minutes apart. They seemed pleased with how everything was going and told Linda and me to hang tight as soon as a room opened, that Mollie would be transferred out to a labor and delivery room. Within an hour or so we found ourselves following Mollie and the triage nurse down a series of empty long hallways to her labor and delivery room. After what seemed about a 10 minute zigzag trip through the somber maze of hospital hallways, Mollie was wheeled into her room.

The room was quite large and was equipped with most of the comforts of a home bedroom. There was a television, a computer desk hookup, a bathroom and all the hospital apparatus that would possibly be needed for the labor and delivery including a bed for

~ Buckle Your Chin Strap ~

Brayden when he arrived, equipped with electric heat coils and lights. It was decorated in a cheery baby theme with all sorts of bright colors. Little did we know when Mollie was wheeled into this room shortly before 8:00 a.m., that we would be spending the next 12+ hours together in this room.

Once the nurses got Mollie settled into her labor and delivery room, we breathed a sigh of relief. We felt that Mollie was now on her way to delivering her baby and would be finished in a few more hours. Suddenly, as quickly as we had breathed our sigh of relief, we were jolted back to the edge of our seats. The door to Mollie's room opened and there in front of us were Johnny and his parents. Brayden's father and his parents were standing before us and Linda and I were shocked, upset and in a fit of rage. Johnny's mother was one of the boldest and most insensitive people I had ever met. She had been calling our house every day the last week of Mollie's pregnancy to monitor what was happening in her progress. She knew that Mollie was having back labor and had called us that morning early after Mollie had text messaged her son Johnny to tell him she was in back labor and that we were taking her in. I could not understand how a woman, who did not believe that my daughter had told the truth that her son was the father, could be so bold and assumptive. I had been praying for weeks for the Lord to hold my tongue and strengthen me for this battle, as I could feel it coming. How could she insist on being there and constantly pestering us when in her mind, the baby might not be her sons? Should I let her stay on the sideline when it was obvious she wasn't totally committed and in the game? After all, from our first meeting she had insisted they wanted to "just make sure." They wanted to get a paternity test. It took all of the Lord's strength for me to hold my tongue and from physically blowing a gasket. Believe me, I wanted to grab them each by the neck and throw

~ Page 116 ~

them out of the room. I wanted to tell them they needed to leave the hospital and after the paternity test was confirmed, we would see about them seeing their son's child. My cousin Debbie had given me the good advice to let all the decisions be Mollie's. As much as I wanted to throw them out of the hospital, I had to yield to Mollie. Mollie wanted Johnny to be there, despite their lack of trust in her. She knew that he was the father and set aside her pride to do the right thing. She wanted Johnny there and if Johnny wanted his parents there, it was okay with Mollie. She taught me a lot about forgiveness in this act, something I needed to do, but was too prideful to attain. I truly believe that this act of forgiveness is something that I believe will be part of Mollie's legacy to her son.

Thankfully, the Lord answered my prayers and He sent his Holy Spirit to calm me and hold my tongue. We greeted them and chitchatted for five minutes or so, as they visited with Mollie in between her contractions. Finally, I said, "Well you guys should wait out in the lobby as Mollie needs to focus on the task at hand." They reluctantly left the room, but were somewhat gracious. Johnny's father, Karl, seemed to be a nice guy. He was reserved and I could tell he felt awkward. I think his wife was used to getting her way on things. He should have put his foot down on this situation. This gave me insight into the legal challenges we would later face. Once they had left the room, I pulled Linda aside and told her that one of us needed to stay at Mollie's side at all times. I did not trust this woman and neither did Linda. I knew from her methods of operation in our meetings that she was used to getting her way and that she would try her best to weasel her way into seeing the baby born. She was accustomed to babying her baby (Johnny) and would want to get him in on the action regardless of how bold she needed to be.

I can honestly say, had the tables been reversed and her son had been Mollie and Mollie had been Johnny, things would have been MUCH different. For starters, if my son had gotten a girl pregnant, I would have left a paternity test decision up to him. If my son had been 18 years old as their son was, he would have been an adult in my eyes. I probably would have encouraged him to do a paternity test since I would not have known the girl either, just as they had not known our Mollie. The decision would have been his though, not mine. From talking with Mollie, Johnny had confided to her that he knew he was the father, but his mom was insistent on a paternity test. This told me a lot about her and a lot about her son. In any event, if the tables were turned and had my son insisted on a paternity test, there is absolutely no way I would've been calling daily for updates on Mollie's condition. Nor would have my son, my wife or I been up at the hospital. I would have had much more class than this. I would have been in the game, before I would have been so bold to come and stand on the sidelines. However, God makes everyone differently and the James were cut from a different set of cloth.

One of the most difficult things to do for your daughter is let her make all the decisions in the pregnancy journey. She knew that Johnny was the father. She wanted him at the hospital despite his parent's insensitivity. She forgave them. We had to forgive them too. If Mollie had wanted Johnny to be there, even in the delivery room, we would have had to let her make the decision.

As quickly as my blood pressure had risen, it subsided when a couple hours later my oldest daughter Amber arrived at the hospital. Amber was our first born and was teaching first grade in Orlando, Florida. When she graduated from Grand Valley State, the Michigan economy and teaching market was at an all time low.

She had gotten an offer to teach school in Orlando and move there at the start of the teaching year. Mollie had wanted her older sister Amber, her mom and me to be the only ones allowed in the labor and delivery room. We had called Amber on Wednesday afternoon telling her that Mollie was in labor. We purchased an airline ticket online Wednesday evening for her to fly home on the first available flight back to Detroit. We did not know if she would make it on time, but were so happy that she arrived in time to witness the miracle of life. Her best friend since fourth grade, Megan, had picked her up and was her taxi service from the airport. Mollie was very happy to see Amber as were we, and the Lord had seen to it that she arrived on time and safely. Our son Steven soon showed up as well. He was two hours away in his junior year of college at Western Michigan University in Kalamazoo, Michigan. Mollie was too embarrassed to have Steven see the miracle, but she was glad to know he was there and waiting just outside the room. I don't think Steven really wanted to witness this anyway. He hung out in the lobby with my older sister Liz who had also come to support us.

While we were in the room helping Mollie, Linda and I would periodically step outside to walk past the lobby to make cellular telephone calls. The cell phones would not work unless you would walk through a maze of corridors to a hall that had large windows. When you stood by these windows, the signal would be strong enough to make calls. Each time one of us would walk through the lobby on the way to this area in which to make a cell phone call, sure as instinct had told us, Johnny's mother would try to sneak back inside of Mollie's labor and delivery room. She would make it look as if she was just trying to check on Mollie, but I knew better. I knew she wanted to have her son and her witness the birth.

Finally, after one of these episodes where Linda had walked out to take a cell phone break, I had to lay down the law. She walked into the room with her son Johnny. Then she asked the question I knew she had wanted to ask when Linda and I were not there. She looked at Mollie and said, "Who is going to be in the room when the baby is born?" At the time I had been sitting in a lounge chair beside Mollie's bed. I immediately sprang to my feet and before Mollie could say anything, I jumped in front of her. I told her it was time to leave. I told her that as Mollie had always communicated the only people who she wanted in the room when the baby was born were her mom, her sister and me. No one else would be allowed in. I asked her to leave and not return. By this point, Mollie was dilated to 8 cm and the contractions were starting to get very painful. This woman had to be one of the most audacious, insensitive, selfish persons I had ever met. I wanted to smack her, but knew that would not help the situation. It was all I could do to hold my tongue and escort her and her son to the door.

As she left the room, she turned and said, "Well, if we can't be in here when the baby is born, Johnny wants to be in the room right away. Right after the baby is born, he wants to be in the room right away!" I simply shook my head yes, but by then my heart was in my throat and my eyes were wide and steaming with wrath. She went on to demand, "And I want him in here before anyone else is allowed in this room, that means before your son or your sister, too!" At this point my wrath had boiled to the point of ERUPTION. How could this woman be so demanding? What right does she have to make such demands when she wanted a paternity test? Why was she doing all her son's talking? Where was her son when my darling little girl had to walk the high school halls alone and pregnant? Who is she to make any such demands?

Does she not know who she was talking about? My sister was Mollie's godmother and had been there for Mollie her entire life. Her brother was her only brother there and the two of them were close as well. Her son on the other hand had vanished when my daughter needed him most and now because his mommy wanted him there, she was making incredulous demands.

After all these fiery one-sided demands, I simply looked at her with the same glare I gave to the Northern Michigan football players who had made fun of St. Jude. I buckled my chin strap and the Holy Spirit held my tongue. She turned and left and I once again took a big breath and breathed a sigh of relief. When Linda returned, I told her briefly what transpired, but did not elaborate until later about the exchange of pleasantries. I knew it would just infuriate her too, and our attention and focus needed to be on the miracle that was in progress. Also, we needed to help our daughter. It was not the last time Cathy James would infuriate me.

The medical staff had given Mollie an epidural which is an anesthetic to block much of the pain. They had waited until she was far enough along with her dilation, because they were fearful that if they gave it to her too soon, that the contractions would subside and her dilation would stop progressing. It was now about 6:00 p.m. and Mollie was still between 8 and 9 cm. We had begun to wonder if she would deliver her son on her birthday after all or not. It had taken 12 hours and she had only gotten to just over 8 cm. A woman's cervix is supposed to be dilated to 10 centimeters before they are allowed to start pushing the baby through the birth canal. Mollie was starting to get a little restless, but still she never complained.

I stepped out of the room one final time to make a last phone call to my father. I wanted to give him an update and ask for his prayers. When I stepped out, I wandered past the lobby and saw my sister, but my son Steven was nowhere in sight. My sister told me that he was so nervous he had to go outside and go for a walk.

This time when I returned to the room, Dr. Morgan had arrived. She was true to her promise to Mollie and was going to be there to deliver Brayden even though it was her day off. She thought she could help Mollie with some position changes to expedite the dilation. Thankfully, an hour or so later, it worked. At approximately 7:00 p.m. she had reached 10 cm. Now she could start pushing during the contractions. "We are in the home stretch now," I thought. But soon, I would learn that Mollie had almost two hours of pushing yet to do, as Brayden was born at 8:47 p.m. on April 18.

As Mollie began her pushing, I would pray the Divine Mercy Rosary and get a cold washcloth and hold it on her head between each contraction. The nurses and Dr. Morgan were so tender and calm. It was amazing to see Dr. Morgan in action; she was quietly confident and assertive in her directions to Mollie for the two hours of pushing. Linda was the opposite. She was barking loud orders and was like a proud coach yelling to her star player with constant reminders of breathing technique and encouragement. It was quite different for Linda to finally be a spectator or coach rather than the player delivering the baby. She was awesome for Mollie!  Amber was quiet like me, however, in the last half hour she became a clone of her mother. With two coaches loudly screaming words of encouragement, me praying repeatedly the Divine Mercy Rosary, and Dr. Morgan's repeated calm but assertive directives, I am amazed that Mollie never once uttered a word of anger or resentment. Not even a request to shut up. She simply was a trooper! In fact, she had been remarkable in comparison to my first such experience with Linda delivering Amber some 24 years earlier. Mollie did what she was told. She never complained, she never uttered a curse word. She never screamed. She never even gave an indication that she was in pain. She endured this pushing for two hours and a total of 52 hours of labor without so much as a whimper.

This was my daughter who three years earlier would cry uncontrollably when I coached her in soccer. Whenever she would get hit by a soccer ball or kicked in the shin, the flood gates would open and she would be sobbing her eyes out. I was truly amazed and told her so afterwards. I whispered in her ear after Brayden was born that she was now one of my heroes!

When Brayden Michael Williams was born, he started to cry a little with a few soft whimpers. Then they put him on the top of Mollie's chest. We all held hands and were crying in pure joy. I silently gave thanks to the Lord for the miracle of Brayden's life. I was asked by Dr. Morgan to cut the cord. I had never gotten the opportunity to do this with any of my four children, since they were delivered by caesarean section. It was an honor. As the nurse handed me the scissors, I gazed over at Mollie. She was so happy. I do not think I have ever seen her look so happy before in my lifetime. Then I glanced over at Linda and Amber who were hugging and sobbing uncontrollably. Here I was, about to cut my grandson's cord with the three girls in my life that mean the most to me. How much more blessed could I be? As I positioned the scissors between the two clamps, I was struck with the irony in what I was about to do. Once I cut the cord, Brayden would no longer be depending on his mother for the substances of life, food, nutrients, oxygen, blood and warmth. I would be in essence setting him free to live and grow in this world on his own. I would also be setting Mollie free from the pregnancy responsibility of providing a safe, warm environment for Brayden to grow and develop. I thought of how many times in our lives God allows us to cut the cord. Sometimes we choose or cut the cord to the road that leads to life and fulfillment, while other times we choose to not cut the cord and it leads to death, disappointment and/or destruction. God gave us all a free will. We are allowed along our journey of earthly life to make these cut the cord decisions. By cutting the cord, I would be setting both Mollie and Brayden free to continue to make these decisions. At the same time, I couldn't help but wonder about all the children who were not given the chance to cut the cord, because their mothers had been deceived into having an abortion. These children would never get the chance to cut their own cords in life, because their mothers had murdered them. Some intentionally, some unknowingly, and some forced by parents who think it is best for them and for their teenage daughters. I silently thanked God for my daughter Mollie and her choosing life for Brayden. As I cut the cord, the blood spewed out for a moment, and then both Mollie and Brayden were freed.

*John Chapter 5 Verse 14 & 15*
*"We have this confidence in Him, that if we ask*
*anything according to His will, He hears us, and if we*
*know that He hears us in regard to whatever we ask,*
*we know that what we have asked Him for is ours."*

Throughout Mollie's pregnancy journey to the miracle of life, I repeatedly had to, "Have confidence in Him." As the father of a teenage pregnant daughter, the journey was difficult, but I had confidence in Him. I knew that my confidence in Him would help me to ask for the proper thing I needed to help me lead my family through this journey. As long as I asked for these things according to His will, I would receive the grace I needed. He would reward my confidence in Him by sending these things via His Holy Spirit. He did that and much more.

I prayed for grace when confronted with "the news" after spending two weeks in Paradise. He sent it. I prayed for clarity in Mollie's decisions all along the way and He sent that as well. I prayed for perseverance while she was 16 and pregnant and attending high school. He sent that not only for me, but more importantly for Mollie. I prayed for strength and understanding without condemnation in the meeting and subsequent visits with Brayden's paternal grandparents. He gave me that too, albeit it might not have been the type of understanding I had hoped for. Finally, I had prayed for protection all along for Mollie and her baby until the miracle of life could be witnessed as we did on Mollie's 17th birthday on April 18, 2007. It will undoubtedly be a birthday unlike any other one she will have in her lifetime. However, it will be a birthday where she can look back and realize that it was God's gift to her and to her son Brayden to share this date together throughout their earthly journeys. The Lord does bless those who bless Him. By listening to His Holy Spirit and choosing life, Mollie was given the most precious gift one could ever receive on their birthday. It was a miracle. "Brayden Michael Williams" a "miracle of life!"

# Chapter 7
# Coming Home

*Matthew Chapter 7 Verse 7 & 8*
*"Ask and it will be given to you, seek and you will find;*
*knock and the door will be opened to you. For everyone*
*who asks, receives; and the one who seeks finds; and*
*the one who knocks the door will be opened."*

As a father of a teenage daughter who became pregnant, these verses in Matthew could be an ongoing theme song of the pregnancy journey. Throughout Mollie's pregnancy, I found myself continually asking, seeking and knocking to the Lord. Additionally, I had to ask for strength and understanding. Not just for me either, but also for my wife Linda. I had to ask Him for the words and His wisdom to communicate to all the people in my life; my family, my friends as well as to Brayden's father's family. I asked Him for help for Mollie in the pregnancy, all her high school activities and in her labor and delivery. I asked Him to grant me forgiveness for both Johnny and his parents' attitudes. I continue to ask Him for His help each and every day now as a grandfather and father helping my daughter through this difficult but fulfilling challenge.

I also found that I sought the Lord more than ever before as I battled all the emotions of the journey. In addition to my daily prayer journal, which I have done faithfully for the past 14 years, I joined a Men's Faith Sharing Group at my church. I also began going online every day and reading the daily readings and responsorial psalms within the Bible. I really sought the Lord and found Him in all the people He brought into my life. Three of my customers had the same thing happen to them and they shared their individual experiences with me once I opened up to them. One of my customers provided and continues to provide insight into the father's family perspectives and how they felt when their son got his girlfriend pregnant. By seeking the Lord in His words, God brought clarity with how I should respond to all the situations, emotions and challenges that a teenage daughter's pregnancy can bring. He helped me deal with my daughter being frightened, afraid, hurt, and lonely. He helped me with my wife and her anger, her bitterness, resentment, fear and continued doubts. By seeking the Lord, you will find Him in the ways you sometimes least expect. I saw Him every day in the people He put in my life. I sought Him out and found Him and now I continue to find Him as my grandson lives in my home with me each day.

Finally, I knocked on the Lord's door each and every day. When you go to a door and knock, you have to prepare for what you may be confronted with once the door opens and you walk inside. When you knock on that door and it is opened, you need to prepare yourself for what God may show you once you come inside. Sometimes it may not be what you thought you would see or what you wanted to see. But if you knock on the door, He opens it and He will show you what you need to see. He showed me that we were not the first family to undergo such a trial. The more people I opened up to, the more I learned that teenage pregnancy happens to almost every family somewhere within their circle of life. Society tends to ignore it or try to fix it by handing out condoms at school and then pretend it does not exist. Teenage girls and their families get pregnant every day. Many of the girls are terrified that their fathers/mothers or even their boyfriends will kill them if they find out. Many of the girls take matters into their own hands and choose to end their baby's life by abortion or taking the RU486 morning after pills. Most of the girls do not desire to murder their children, but they feel like they have no one to support or help them. Many of the girls, actually 70% of them, do not even graduate from high school if they choose to have the child. Less than 1% of those who do graduate from high school move on and attend college. If they make the right choice after they make a poor one, which is to give their baby life after engaging in premarital sex, their lives are sentenced to poverty, misery and financial hardship.

God has shown me that although this is a problem and will continue to be a problem, there is a solution. It is not a cure-all solution. It is a solution that will help. Most of the girls who get pregnant as teenagers who choose to have the babies do not have moms and dads who can help them. They need help to raise their children, or the willingness to sacrifice in order to help their child. Many of the teenage girls are from single-parent and/or broken home families whose parents are struggling financially to even support them. However, if these girls had a resource to help them help themselves, many of them would choose life and choose responsibility. They need hope. They would choose responsibility for themselves and their child. But they would never be successful without help from someone close to them.

That is why I am going to create a foundation to help poor pregnant teenage girls. The mission of the foundation will be to help pregnant teenagers choose life and choose responsibility for themselves and their child. The foundation will be set up to give those teenage girls help. Help of daycare. Help with counseling. Help of diapers, formula, and food. Help with education and college. The foundation will start small and eventually build and grow to help these girls help themselves. Someday, Lord willing, I hope to build daycare centers where these girls can bring their babies to be cared for while they pursue their education, jobs, and careers. The daycare centers will be staffed by volunteer retired adoptive/foster grandparents/aunts/uncles who can offer care for the children who need care while their mothers get their educations.

I have promised the Lord that if this book gets published, any money it makes will be deposited into the foundation. In order for the foundation to work, though, it will need help. Help from people like you who read this book. People who care about life and care about making a difference in the world we live in. The foundation will be named "Michael's Wings" so that like Michael the arch-angel it can spread its wings to give protection, shade from the parching sun, and help to these teenage pregnant girls along with protection to their unborn children. The Lord showed me what I needed to see about myself, my daughter, my wife and society when I knocked on His door. I will continue to knock on His door every day and ask Him to show me what I need to see as I journey through the remainder of this wonderful life journey.

After Mollie and our family experienced the miracle of Brayden's life, we began to prepare for Mollie and Brayden's homecoming. In the months that led up to the birth, we had begun to prepare our home for a new baby. Linda and Mollie redecorated my oldest daughter Amber's room who is out on her own now, into a nursery. We had to find a crib, a changing table, repaint, all the typical things you do for a new baby's room. As we prepared for the coming home of our grandson, I found myself reflecting often on the various homecomings I had experienced in my life. I thought of all four of our children and the excitement and anxiety we felt from Amber my oldest, to our two boys Steven and Michael in the middle, to Mollie our youngest child. In each case, we prepared our home for the child's coming home. These were the most exciting times of my life.

I thought about the times I would come home from college in my four years away at Grand Valley State and how my parents treated me as well as my brothers and sisters. Each time they stopped what they were doing to let me know they were excited that I was finally back home. When they did this it made me feel like I belonged and was loved which is something all of us need to feel.

I thought of all the homecomings I had attended at Grand Valley State University. As a season ticket holder since graduating in 1979, Linda and I managed to attend most of the Homecoming football games despite all the activities that our kids were involved in, we always tried to get back for Homecoming. We were always excited to go home, see our family and friends while reliving old memories and creating new ones. Home is the greatest place on earth to be.

I also thought a lot about those whom I loved who went home for eternity. I thought of my mother Janet who left us to go home to the Lord on November 30, 1995 at the age of 60. She died of a heart attack less than three months after an early retirement. I thought of Linda's mom Ruth who had passed away only a year ago March 23, 2006 at the age of 81 after battling cancer and osteoporosis. I thought of many of my friends who had died at young ages from tragic accidents like Barb Rogge, Daryl Gooden, Danny Jackson, Corky Meinecke, Jan Walz, Jim Crowley and countless others. What was it like to be finally home? Jesus told us he went to prepare a place for us in His father's house. How did Jesus feel now that they were home? How did they feel? How will I feel when I finally go home for eternity?

When you prepare for someone to come home that you love, it can be an invigorating feeling. When you are the person who goes home, it is a very exciting feeling as well. While I was away at college my freshman year, I went home every weekend that first autumn football season. I could not wait to be home where I felt safe and loved. I could relax, eat my mother's home-cooked meals and enjoy my visits with my brothers and sisters. I have two brothers: Dave who is two years younger than me and Joe who is three years younger. Both Dave and Joe followed me to Grand Valley State where they both were involved with the football program, too. Dave and I were starting offensive guards my last two years and Joe was a student assistant coach. My three sisters are Lizzie who is the oldest in the family and firstborn, Lorie who is six years younger than me and Judy the baby 10 years younger. We all grew up in a one bathroom home with four bedrooms on Hamilton Street in Jackson, Michigan. Whenever I would go home that first year in college and subsequent years, I would get butterflies in my belly. I loved my brothers and sisters and my parents and couldn't wait to get home.

Now that Brayden was coming home I wondered what his life would be like. What will his home be like? Will he feel like his grandparent's home is his home? Will his mother be able to provide a home for him eventually on her own? What will he feel like when he is my age when he reflects on home? Questions like these raced through my mind as Linda and I drove to the hospital early that morning to pick Brayden and Mollie up and bring them both "HOME."

As we drove to the hospital, Linda and I wondered together what our lives would be like with a baby in our house again. Neither one of us were quite sure if we could handle nightly feedings again, the crying of an infant and the unrest that a baby can create in a home. We were determined to help, but we did not want to make it easy for our daughter. It was her choice and she needed to accept the full consequences of her decision.

We pulled up to the hospital that sunny April morning and parked the car in the baby pickup zone. Then we rode the elevator to the seventh floor to pick up our daughter and grandson. As Linda and I rode the large chrome plated elevator up, the butterflies of excitement churned in my belly once again. It was at this moment that I knew everything would be okay with a baby in our home once again. I knew that these butterflies were God's sign that everything would be just fine. I remembered that these were the same butterflies I had felt when I brought each of my children home. They were also the same ones I felt when I would travel home to see my parents and before every football game I ever played in high school and college. Butterflies were a good thing! They are God's sign that you care. When you care about something, you will put forth the maximum effort you need to deliver the type of results you hope for. In all my years of competing on the gridiron, I've never experienced one game for which butterflies were absent. That told me that I cared. I knew that if I cared, everything would be fine. So this was God's sign to me that yes I did care and He would make sure everything worked out just fine.

Speaking of butterflies, my butterfly stories would not be complete if I did not tell you about my ultimate experience with butterflies. Not butterflies in my stomach either. "REAL" butterflies. The kind that fly in the air!

Three weeks after Linda and I had returned from Hawaii, we flew to Victoria Island, British Columbia in Canada. I had qualified for a sales trip for my company that year, and it was a four-day trip. We flew there and enjoyed Victoria Island for a long weekend. During the last day of our trip, we decided to rent a car and drive all around the perimeter of the island to take in the sights, since our flight did not leave until late in the day. Victoria Island is magnificent, colorful and has many old Victorian homes built along the seashore. I have never been to Maine or Cape Cod, but I was told that Victoria Island's coastline is similar to these places. There were a lot of quaint fishing wharfs, and big old homes through rolling terrains and even some cliffs.

At one point in our trip, we saw a "Butterfly Gardens" sign. We decided to stop and check it out. It was a huge greenhouse filled with butterflies, exotic plants and even running fresh water streams. As we entered the greenhouse area, there were thousands of plants, hundreds or trees, ornate shrubs, and even fish stocked ponds and running manmade streams inside. The greenhouse provided a year-round habitat for hundreds of species of butterflies.

After about 15 minutes inside the Garden, I had seen enough, (the guys reading this I am sure would agree), and told my wife so. You could only handle so many butterfly signs and tour guides talking about butterflies. My wife was listening to one of the tour guides, when I wandered off to the opposite side of the greenhouse, over in a corner near the exit doors. Suddenly, as I was merely standing there daydreaming, there were about a dozen or so people gathering around me and their cameras were clicking. I did not understand what all the commotion was about. Did they think I was a celebrity of some kind? Obviously, they had mistaken me for someone else. Finally, an elderly gentleman with an eastern accent ordered me to stand still, "Keep standing still young man," he yelled. It seemed that there was a large blue

Morpheus butterfly on my left shoulder and his wings were spread outright so that you could photograph and see the bright blue color of his wings. I did not know or realize why this was such a fuss until I later learned that Blue Morphs rarely show their blue interior side of their wings to be photographed. When and if they land, most of the time their wings are in a closed position and upright with only the black outer colorings visible. This BLUE butterfly was on my shoulder for at least three or four minutes and the crowd soon grew to twenty or 30 people each clicking their cameras. Finally my wife Linda made it over and snapped a couple shots, too. Right after Linda snapped her pictures, the BLUE butterfly flew away. At the time, I did not realize the significance of this, nor did I understand it. When we returned home, I soon found out the significance of this experience and what it really meant.

When we got home from Victoria Island, we learned from a friend exactly how rare it is to get a picture of a BLUE Morph with the blue wings visible. She told us that a blue morph would be eaten by predators in their natural habitat if they did not keep their wings closed and in an upright position. She also told us that it was a biblical sign, something about God was watching over you. At the time she told us this, our friend did not know that our daughter Mollie was pregnant. After she told Linda and me this, we looked at each other with the undeniable revelation that she was right. It was God's sign to us that He was sending His Holy Spirit to our family to watch over us and our Mollie through her pregnancy journey. He was trying to tell us that He would be there through it all. He would be with us even through Mollie's labor and delivery into the raising of her son. How blessed we were to come to that revelation.

As the elevator doors opened, the butterflies were still churning and I thought of this blue butterfly. He was still there on my left shoulder to signify that the Lord was right there looking over me, from my shoulder, watching and helping me, my daughter, my wife and family. Now I had butterflies in my stomach and one on my shoulder as I headed to Mollie's hospital room to bring her and Brayden Michael Williams home. I now have a blue Morpheus butterfly mounted in a plastic box and perched on the bathroom tub in our master bathroom. Each night I am able to give my grandson Brayden a bath, I look at that BLUE butterfly and smile knowing that God's Holy Spirit is still here watching over my daughter, my grandson and my family.

When I got to her room, Mollie had a phenomenal and unforgettable glow on her face. She had completed the pregnancy, the labor, the delivery and now she was coming home. She was coming home to her home with her son Brayden in her arms. I don't know if she had butterflies in her stomach, but I will never forget that bright soft glow on her face and the sparkle in her eyes. Brayden and his mommy, my Mollie, were coming home. I had always told Mollie that it does not matter how big or how small your house is, it just matters how much love there is inside. I knew from Mollie's glow and sparkle that she knew there was plenty of love inside her home. Surely there was enough for a new addition. Our first grandchild, Brayden Michael Williams. They both coming home.

*First Peter Chapter 1 Verse 6 & 7*
*"And if you rejoice, although for a little while you may*
*have to suffer through various trials, so that the*
*genuineness of your faith, more precious than gold that*
*is perishable even though tested by fire, they proved to*

*be for praise, glory and honor at the revelation of Jesus Christ. "*

Now that my daughter Mollie has made it back home through the trials of the pregnancy at 16 and through the labor and delivery of her son Brayden, we could truly rejoice. For eight months, we suffered through the storms together over pregnancy and all the doubts, fears, and all those armchair quarterbacks who always have all the answers giving us advice (when it was not their daughter). With the Lord's help, we persevered. Our faith was more precious than gold. It is perishable. However, only through the grace of Jesus Christ did our faith survive the fire of teenage pregnancy. Now because we trusted in the Lord, our faith is actually stronger. We all know that we now have a living testimony to the praise, glory and honor of Jesus Christ. The testimony and revelation is Mollie's son Brayden. God has a special plan for Brayden and his life just like He does for each of us. Now that Brayden is here and among us, Jesus will reveal that in the time that He chooses. The most important thing is that we were obedient to His call. We stood for life and Mollie took the difficult road knowing that we would be there to help her. Through God's grace, we were tested in this difficult teenage pregnancy journey, but now we can see that it was truly for the praise and glory of His name. I truly thank God that Mollie had the courage to choose life for Brayden.

# Chapter 8
## The Return to School

*Isaiah Chapter 50 Verse 7*
*"The Lord God is my help therefore I am not disgraced;*
*I have set my face like flint, knowing that I shall not be*
*put to shame."*

Can you imagine what it would be like to return to high school in eleventh grade less than four weeks after having a child? Physically and emotionally it would be a challenge that I believe few could endure. But mentally it would be quite daunting as well. The stares from classmates you would receive. The whispers, the snickering, and the finger-pointing you would receive in the school hallways and at lunchroom tables. The ache you would have in your arms to hold and be with your child. Not to mention the stress from being a first-time mom and all the responsibilities that go with it. Although society says that unwed mothers are a disgrace and an abomination to the social norm, Mollie had the Lord God to help her. She did set her face like flint as hard as quartz, and she knew that she was not going to be put to shame. Her help came from the Lord and she made a courageous choice to return to her regular high school, when it would have been easier to choose the Alternative Education Schools.

Living in a fairly affluent school district, Mollie had several options from which she could choose to return to high school. She could have chosen to drop out of her second semester of her junior year in high school and go to summer school to repeat her Junior second semester. This did not seem like a good option to either Mollie or my wife and me. That would have put her idle at home from January through July with the baby due in April; we both knew that this would not be good. Luckily for us, Mollie made another good decision. She wanted to continue to go to school while pregnant and resume school as soon as possible right after the baby was born. She also could have chosen to enter two alternative education schools upon her return from the birth, one run by our school district, and the other one run by the county we live in. Although the alternative education schools would have allowed her to bring her baby to school and utilize daycare resources at the alternative education sites, Mollie was not comfortable with this situation either. She did not want her baby to be exposed to a lot of others at the peak of the cold and flu season in Michigan and have someone watching and caring for the child whom she did not know or trust. She also did not want to leave her friends.

If she had chosen the alternative education route, she would have graduated on her own in a private ceremony, without any of her friends with whom she had grown up with and shared her life. She wanted to walk with her classmates and friends. My wife Linda and I went back and forth on this. Part of us knew that we could not make it easy on Mollie and she would not always have an easy road. But in looking at the other part, we did see her logic in the stranger caring for her child part and the increased exposure and risks to colds and flu if her child went to the alternative education daycare center.

Naturally, we wanted her to be able to keep her friends and graduate with them. But if we let her do this, who would care for the baby? Linda worked a full-time job as a Para-professional at a local elementary school and we used her health-care benefits, since my company offered a more expensive and less service-based health care plan. We would not only need the benefits for the baby, but for the rest of our family and for our retirement health care benefits. She also loved her job and it made virtually little or no sense for her to quit to watch our grandson. What were we going to do? Who would be able to watch Brayden?

Thankfully, our help and Mollie's help came from the Lord in the form of one of his earthly angels in Kristen Pertler. Kristen was one of Mollie's best friend's mom and she volunteered to watch Brayden. Once Mollie returned to school after having her son, in her junior year, Kristen would not allow us to pay her and refused to take a cent for babysitting. She was an angel of mercy to Mollie, Brayden and our entire family. Kristen had three daughters one in high school, one in junior high and one in elementary school. So you can imagine how busy her life already was with all the demands of three daughters in three levels of school. Morgan, who is Kristen's daughter, told us that her mom had contemplated looking for a job, but she gave that up and sacrificed in her love for our daughter Mollie.

She told us that she felt that the Lord was calling her to help Mollie and our family out. It was only through persistent coaxing that we were able to convince Kristen to accept a modest weekly fee for her help in caring for Brayden during Mollie's senior year. We took Kristen's love offering as a sign from the Lord that Mollie should stay on course as a normal high school student and graduate with her class at her regular high school. This was another example to me that our God walks in His servants dwellings. As busy as Kristen was raising three daughters, she was God's instrument of mercy and love to our family. I know as a father/grandfather how much I appreciated this. I am sure Mollie appreciates it now, but one day when she is older and wiser, she will look back and be overwhelmed with how Kristen was really being Jesus to her, in her time of great need.

After Brayden was born, we had arranged through Mollie's classmates and friends and/or e-mail from her teachers to receive Mollie's daily assignments for each of her classes on a weekly basis. The teachers at Mollie's high school were another sign that the Lord was Mollie's help. They were phenomenal. Each teacher whom she had a class with, went out of their way to either e-mail the assignments or they made sure to send the assignments home with one of Mollie's friends. It was Mollie's responsibility to complete the assignments and return them to the teachers every week. She needed to stay on task in order to stay home for four weeks after Brayden was born.

Technically, we learned that homebound services were not allowed for pregnancies since a pregnancy was not considered a disability. However, through the help of Mollie's counselor Mrs. Brunch, and some wonderful kindhearted teachers, a compromise was made. Was this lucky? Yes you may say this, but it really was a result of receiving God's grace to work for what it was we were praying for. Mollie, together with Linda and me as her parents, had to be assertive and meet with counselors, teachers and school administrators to work out this compromise. We did not sit back and let the problem attack us. We attacked the problem. We buckled our chin straps and played the next play. Each play was one play at a time. We went after it before it came after us. That is how you win football games and it is also how you win the battle of teenage pregnancy.

In football, I learned that if you want to play the game well, you need to practice hard and commit yourself to do whatever it takes to get the job done. My high school coach always told us that we will play in the games how we practice. If we practice with intensity and effort, then that is how we will play come Saturday night game time. If we practice going through the motions with little or lackluster effort, then that is how we will play come Saturday night at game time. The choice really was ours. What choice would we make?

As a small offensive guard in college, I frequently blocked opponent's defensive tackles that outweighed me by 50 to 100 pounds. The only way I could be successful was to outwork, out prepare, out think, and out hustle my opponents. Although they were bigger, often stronger, and sometimes faster, I could play well enough to do my job if I prepared for my assignment that week. Part of the assignment might mean watching extra film on my own of my opponent to study their defensive schemes, tendencies and techniques. Sometimes it meant staying after and working on the little things like my first step, pulling, bounce blocks, cut offs, peel backs, pass blocking, chop blocking, and play action pass blocking. Sometimes it meant lifting extra weights in the weight room after practice when tired. By doing this weight lifting when your body was tired after a full day's practice, it would train my muscles and mind that I could still perform when tired or exhausted. In most games that I played while in college at Grand Valley State, I was usually in much better shape than my opponents were by the fourth quarter and end of a football game. This helped me accomplish my assignments easier despite the size differential I usually had against me. It was because I believed in the St. Thomas Moore philosophy which he always preached, "You should pray for the grace to work for that which you pray for." I was also taught this same philosophy by my father as well as my high school football coach Jim Crowley.

I was fortunate to have a teammate who played on the offensive line with me at Grand Valley State who epitomized this philosophy in his work ethic. His name was Ron Essink. In college, Ron was brought in as a 6' 7", 190 lb little known tight end out of Zeeland, Michigan. Ron was hurt in his high school senior football season and did not play much that last year of high school. However, he decided as a senior in high school after a disappointing football season, to take up the sport of wrestling. Having never wrestled before, and then participating in it for the first time as a senior, he thought he would be fortunate if he even made first-team for his high school wrestling team. Through hard work, he earned the first team heavyweight wrestler, despite only weighing 190 pounds and wrestling guys much heavier and many times more experienced than him. Ron lost his first high school match that year. However, he did not let that defeat him or discourage him. He used the loss as motivation to go on and work harder in order to win every remaining match that year, eventually becoming the state champion. His individual record that year was 39-1. The odds of someone else being able to achieve this feat, in my opinion are very minute. It would be like getting a hole in one in golf in the first round of golf in your life. In fact, I would doubt if it will ever be done again.

Ron's amazing work ethic and attitude blended with mine on the gridiron, we became good friends and eventually roommates. We were often the last two left on the practice field or weight room working together to prepare us to play well for our team. Eventually, Ron went on to be a two-time national heavyweight champion and an All-American in both football and wrestling in NCAA Division II. He was drafted by the

Seattle Seahawks where he started every game at left offensive tackle for a seven year career. This included his rookie year which is very difficult to do. A left offensive tackle is usually your best athlete on the offensive line and is the most pressure oriented offensive line position, since most teams put their best pass rusher at the right defensive end. Ron was a shining example of St. Thomas Moore's philosophy. He did not just pray to perform well and do well, he worked for it. He worked hard for it and all of his teammates saw and admired it. He was blessed with a lot of talent and size, however, it was his work ethic that propelled him to his success and achievements.

I tell this all to you as a father to let you know that when your teenage daughter gets herself "knocked up" and pregnant, it is not the end of the world. It is a defining moment in your life as a father. Are you going to take the easy way out and demand that your daughter receives or let her choose abortion? Are you willing to work for what you pray for? Are you willing to sacrifice for the sake of the team? Your daughter as well as your wife and other children in your family will look to you and see how you react to her situation. No matter what your relationship is with your daughter, this is an opportunity to move it in a better direction. Seize this opportunity! I promise you that you won't regret it.

On a cold, gray and rainy morning May 14, 2007, Mollie returned to school less than four weeks after giving birth to her son. As she left our house at 6:40 a.m. that morning, I remember praying for her. I asked God to watch over her and help her through the five weeks she had left of her eleventh grade year. I cannot imagine how she felt; leaving her son and returning to school would be tough, no doubt. But to Mollie's credit, she never complained or shed a tear. She simply did what she knew she had to do.

As she drove off to school with her friend Samantha that cold May morning, I ran to the door with Brayden in my arms. We have a tradition in our home to always wave goodbye when someone we love is about to leave on a journey, whether short or far. Brayden and I stood there and waved to his mommy from our front porch. It was as if our waves told Mollie not to worry, everything will be all right.

Over the next five weeks of Mollie's return to school, I had to buckle my chin strap once again and help my daughter. Her school started every morning at 7:00 a.m., and it would have been physically and emotionally draining on Mollie if both Linda and I could not help her with Brayden. The late-night and/or early-morning feedings were no longer just Mollie's. We knew that if Mollie did not get a good night's sleep, she would be exhausted and unable to concentrate on her studies once she was back in school. We came up with a calendar system in which every third night Mollie would have to get up with Brayden for his feedings. The other nights, were shared between Linda and me. Most of the weeks, Mollie would only have one night during the school week to get up. This enabled her to study and focus on her task, but it also did not let her off the hook totally. By her getting up one or two evenings during the week, she would bond with her son and also appreciate the help that we were giving her.

The good news for Linda and me was that this was only temporary. We only had to endure these late-night feedings for five weeks, the rest of her junior year. After that, mommy would be home for summer vacation, and she could resume the feeding duties.

Most evenings Brayden would wake up only once usually between 2:00 or 3:00. However, there were occasions where he would wake up twice usually around 1:00 a.m. and then again at 4:00 a.m. On those nights, the person whose turn it was would be totally wiped out the next day. But we persevered through these five weeks working together as a team!

Since Mollie's school started so early, I also had Brayden duty every morning. I felt it was easier for me since I was a morning person and Linda had to be to school by 8:30 a.m. I usually would wake up around 5:00 a.m. take my shower, iron my clothes, pack Mollie's lunch and do my daily prayer journal and daily Bible readings online. Brayden normally woke up between 6:30 and 7:00 a.m., so I would be all ready prior to when it was time for him to get ready for Kristen's. Most mornings he would wake up happy so it made it much easier. Sometimes though, he would wake up at 5:00 a.m. cranky and that would really put a bump in the road for my routine. When that happened, I would be unable to do my daily prayer journal and Bible readings, since when he woke up, he was usually ready for action for a few hours. The morning routine for Brayden usually consisted of change his diaper, make his bottle, feed and burp him, read him a book or two, then change his clothes for the day. Once his clothes were changed, then I could drive him to Kristen's house, our sitter, and drop him off. Normally, I would drop him off between 7:30 and 8:00 a.m. It was a 15 minute ride to Kristen's house from our home.

In Mollie's subsequent senior year, it would take even longer for the morning routine. During her senior year, I would also need to feed him his yogurt and cereal before leaving the house, in addition to the other routines described earlier. Some days I would be all ready to leave and he would either, spit up on his outfit, have a bowel movement, or spit up on my outfit, causing unexpected and unappreciated delays.

Luckily, these delays were the exception rather than the rule.

As the grandfather now helping get the baby ready for the day at the sitter's house, I found a new appreciation for my wife and what she went through with our first two children. When our first two children were born, Linda would do the morning routine before taking them to the babysitters, so I never understood or appreciated the amount of effort you go through to get children ready for babysitters. I only had to do it for one and I cannot imagine what it would be like to also have another one to get ready as well. Some days I found myself taking a deep sigh and enjoying the long ride to work in silence. Often I reflected though on this experience as a blessing. I was helping my daughter. I was forming a bond with my grandson. It showed me what my wife did in the early years of our marriage and it made me love her and respect her even more!

All things said, it was a great experience. It gave me a sense of appreciation for what unwed mothers must go through daily. It also showed me that teenage moms need a lot of help. I wondered what teenagers did that did not have a parent or parents who were willing to help. I was helping my teenager cope with being a mom, but what about other teens whose fathers/mothers were not there for them? What would they do? How could they continue their education? The answer is that in fact unfortunately 70% of teenage mothers who keep their babies don't even graduate from high school because they receive little or limited support. They are lost and alone with minimal or no help. But one day with the Lord's help this, too, can change.

For now let me first encourage any mother or father reading this to be strong and have faith. Help your daughter if she becomes pregnant. Don't abandon her. Be Jesus to her and to your grandchild. The benefits will far outweigh the sacrifice that you will have to make.

Mollie, through God's grace, completed her junior year on time and on task. Her report card for that semester was an A, four Bs, and one C. This may not seem very impressive to most of you reading this, but to me it was something I was very proud of. To endure the last trimester of pregnancy, work two jobs, give birth, be a mom, do home correspondence studies for a month after birth, return to school, take final exams and achieve a 3.0 GPA was remarkable to me. This is especially true when you consider that prior to Mollie's pregnancy, her first two year high school academic performance was a putrid and less than stellar career GPA of 1.96. It seemed to me that having this child, although it was not the way I would have wished to acquire my first grandchild, was really the event in Mollie's life that pushed her to the next level academically, emotionally and maturity-wise. She now knew that her child was going to be dependent on her getting a good education so that she could eventually support her son herself. Her combined junior year of high school GPA was a 3.33 GPA since she received a 3.67 GPA that first semester of her junior year while pregnant. GOOD can come out of every bad situation with effort and God's grace. Mollie's successful return to school was an event I will always admire in her and be equally thankful to God for having given her the strength to accomplish this important endeavor.

*Hebrews Chapter 2 Verse 18*
*"Because He Himself was tested through what He suffered, He is able to help those who are being tested."*

Throughout our teenage daughter's journey through unwed pregnancy, she was tested and so was I. First, my faith was tested. Did I really accept my role as a Christian father? Could my daughter and the rest of my family see my faith that somehow the Lord will make everything all right? Was I strong enough to stand for the right thing? In times of adversity you get to see a person's true character. What was my character and would I crumble?

Then my marriage and the relationship I have with my wife was tested. It was without a doubt the toughest thing our marriage ever went through. Not once did I blame my wife for Mollie's pregnancy nor did she once blame me, but it was still very difficult. Women and men respond differently to this type of adversity. We were going to have to sacrifice our "golden years" and "empty nester years" to help our daughter. Who knows for how long we would be helping her, but I did not worry about that. Linda restated too many times that we had finally gotten to the point in our lives where we could have "our time" to do what we wanted to do. Just when it appeared that we could see the light at the end of the tunnel, the light vanished. "This just wasn't fair," she constantly reminded me. Now God had a different plan and it was extremely hard for her to accept.

I did not let Satan break up our marriage as he had intended. The two of us are one, and we will stay one. God joined us and made us one on May 2, 1981 and that is the way we will stay until death separates us. We made a covenant with God when we said our vows and I believe that once you do this, it can never be broken until death.

Sometimes offense wins games and sometimes it's defense that wins the games. This was my time in our marriage to step up and win the game, but only through God's grace. I had to play every play offense, defense and special teams once again like I did while in high school never willing to come off the field of play. Satan was there trying to put another wedge in our marriage and there was no way I was going to let him do that to me. I knew that I had the Lord Jesus and His Holy Spirit on my side. Linda my beautiful bride has come a long way, and with God's help she will one day look back on this and see that all being said, it was truly a blessing. It was a blessing which came in disguise which sometimes is the case.

Lastly, we are continually tested by Bradyen's father and his family and the judicial system which is flawed at best. It has cost us much pain, grief and financially more than it should in attorney fees and court costs. But as Hebrew's second chapter points out, Jesus was tested too, by what he suffered. Never did He complain or cry out to His Father. He persevered and triumphed over His sufferings of torture, crucifixion and death on a cross. Now that we were being tested, surely it was His Holy Spirit that helped us get through all these little tests. Sometimes you need to endure suffering and personal challenges so that your faith can grow. Sometimes sufferings come so that you can be God's witness. A witness that His word assures us here in Hebrews Chapter 2 that He helps those who are being tested.

There is absolutely no way Mollie or our family could have gotten through this whole ordeal without Jesus helping us all. As I look back now, I am thankful that through God's grace, He helped Mollie and us endure these tests. In your life at this moment, you may be enduring your own "tests" right now. Please rest assured that through God's grace and faith, He will help you through your test. However, if you want His help in this test, you must ask Him for it. Don't be afraid every day or any time in the day when these tests come, to ask Him in prayer for His help. He helped Mollie and He helped me. He will surely help you because you, too, are His beloved son/daughter!

# Chapter 9
## Summer Vacation?

*James Chapter 1 Verse 2 & 3*
*"Consider it all joy, my brothers and sisters when you encounter various trials, for you know that testing of your faith produces perseverance."*

That first summer with a baby was an eye opening experience for our daughter Mollie. She had been accustomed to being a normal teenager when summer vacation came. She would stay up late at night and sleep until noon in each of her prior high school summers. Those days were now over. With a child, she would go to bed late, but then get up early to feed and care for her son. Sometimes I would see him before I went to work, but I would always wake her up when it was time for me to leave. I am sure Mollie did not consider that first summer vacation as a mom "all joy," like a normal high school teenager did. It was surely a trial for her as it was for our whole family. But it has produced perseverance in her which is worth more than gold.

Mollie's maternal grandfather Clarence L. Gates was a model of perseverance. He grew up poor in Grand Rapids, Michigan, and endured many trials in his lifetime. He persevered through the Great Depression and decided to join the US Navy after graduating from high school. While in the Navy, he fought in World War II and endured some painful experiences. He witnessed seeing a gunner mate get his face ripped off while firing upon enemy ships. He later was blown up by a German submarine when his US Skill Mine Sweeper Ship was torpedoed by the enemy submarine.

He was one of only 25 men out of a crew of over 150 who survived. That day he had been sick to his stomach, so he went up to the bow of the ship to light up a cigarette. After he lit up a cigarette, he woke up floating on a piece of debris in the water with a shipmate who had saved his life and pulled him to the floating debris. There was fire and black smoke everywhere and all his clothes were ripped and burned off his body. He had several shrapnel wounds from the explosions.

Eventually after floating in the sea for several hours, a lifeboat came to pick up the survivors. When it came time to swim from the floating debris to the boat, Clarence's shipmate who saved his life pulling him to the debris helped him swim to the lifeboat. As they swam to the boat, Clarence wondered if they would make it. By now, several sharks had come due to the scent of human blood and they were feasting on human remains and those who were still alive. He saw many of his shipmates eaten alive by the sharks. Regrettably, his shipmate who saved his life was one. As his shipmate pushed him into the lifeboat first, a shark came up suddenly and pulled his shipmate under the sea, never to be seen again.

Clarence was distraught over this for the rest of his life. He could not understand why he was allowed to live while his shipmate, who saved his life twice, was eaten alive by a shark. He battled at least nine bouts of depression after this in his lifetime where he was admitted to hospitals for care. To Clarence's credit, he learned to no longer be prejudiced against any of his brothers here on earth. The man who saved his life was African American.

Clarence also endured the trial of losing his job after 37 years of faithful service at the age of 57. He was terminated and let go as part of a cost savings measure. It was the first wave of downsizing or right sizing in the US industry and occurred around the late 1980s. This company wanted to right-size/downsize in order to eliminate jobs and save costs. Clarence had planned to retire in another five years at age 62. If he would have been allowed to work these additional five years, he would have made 35% more on his $1,200 monthly pension which was not a lot to live on. Clarence felt betrayed and demoralized. How could his company do this to him? He had been a loyal employee for 37 years. I later calculated that the company saved themselves over $3 million in pension costs as 10 of his colleagues all in their late 50s had also been let go.

After this setback, Clarence persevered through losing his hearing. He became totally deaf in one ear and then later deaf in both ears. His last demonstration of perseverance was spending the last nine years of his life in a veteran's home. His wife could no longer meet his needs as he suffered from dementia and depression. In order to keep her sanity, his wife Ruth had to admit him into a home where he could be supervised and properly cared for. Clarence endured these last nine years of his life in the veteran's home and never once complained. I believe that he was a shining example of how to persevere in life when things go wrong.

The first summer with Brayden went by very quickly. Mollie continued to work at the local sandwich restaurant five days a week. Linda and I shared watching over Brayden. We decided to fly in August to see our oldest daughter Amber who was on her summer break as a teacher in Orlando, Florida. Bringing a four month old infant on an airplane was quite an experience. Brayden surprised us all and he did fantastic! He slept most of the ride down and for the entire ride back. Mollie had prepared bottles of formula ahead of time and we fed them to him while on the airplane and we were grateful that he fell asleep. Our visit to Orlando was hot at that time of year, but the change in scenery was a welcome sight. We were all a little stir crazy being locked in a home since April. It was a nice vacation to Orlando.

My best friend during this first summer was Brayden's stroller. I loved to take him on long stroller rides sometimes as long as 90 minutes. The stroller rides would accomplish many things. First, it would be a diversion for Brayden to see his outside world. Second, the stroller rides would give my wife Linda and Mollie a break from Brayden care. Thirdly, they would give me some much needed exercise. I used to run, but due to back problems, knee problems and hip problems, I had to give running up. So the long walks were good for me, too! Lastly, these stroller ride walks helped me have time to be in reflection about the realities of life as a grandfather with a teenager still in high school. As a father, you need to take time for yourself to keep your mind focused on the jobs you must accomplish at home with your daughter, your wife, your family and your grandchild.

Mollie learned that first summer that being a parent is a tremendous responsibility and requires sacrifice. Most of her friends were going out at night "hanging out" and being teenagers. She had to stay home and take care of her child. It was a rude awakening. Linda and I usually gave her one night a week plus a weekend night to do what she wanted and disappear with her friends. She needed time away, too, in order to recharge.

After a long summer, Mollie prepared for her upcoming senior year with another difficult decision. She knew that her son's father would eventually be getting parenting time and she wanted to do what was right for her child. Johnny James had been allowed to come over and visit since the day Brayden came home as long as either Linda or I were home. But Brayden had never been overnight with his dad and that was a scary proposition to consider for both Mollie and my wife Linda. We debated it for several days and after much discussion/evaluation, Mollie decided to allow Johnny to have Brayden every other week and overnight for Friday and Saturday nights through Sunday 6:00 p.m. Mollie decided that this arrangement would be effective on September 1. It was another difficult thing for Mollie to do, but she did it.

Technically, the father still had no visitation rights since he had refused to put his name on the birth certificate and insisted on the paternity test. He was going to have to file a legal action in order to gain paternity as well as change the birth certificate so that his name would appear on it. However, we had to keep reminding ourselves, what was best for their son? How long should he be kept from his father? How long would the legal actions take? Would it have adverse effects on Brayden if the overnight stays were not allowed?

As the father of NOW a teenage unwed mother, and never having had experience traveling down this road, I made what ultimately may have been my biggest mistake. We reluctantly went along with Mollie's decision to give these voluntary visitations to his father, primarily because Mollie and Johnny were now back together as a couple and she thought it would be okay. I must admit that Linda had a bigger problem with allowing these every other weekend visitations to occur than I did. I rationalized that they were a couple. I also rationalized that the court would eventually rule that he gets these visits anyway, so what was the big deal? That way we could at least get the chance to have our life back and be able to do things every other weekend. I later learned that my rationalization could have been a mistake. Always trust the mothers or woman's instincts when it comes to decisions with a child.

Johnny had voluntarily started giving Mollie $100 a month to help with diapers, formula and daycare costs in June and he seemed genuinely interested in being a father. Although it was not much, it was appreciated and taken as a positive sign. He attended all the doctor appointments and appeared to be a potentially good father. The weekend before Mollie agreed to let Johnny start the weekend overnights, I made another difficult decision which may have been another critical mistake. My wife Linda had left for the weekend to spend time with her high school girlfriends. Mollie asked me if she could bring Brayden to Johnny's parents' house to spend the night. She wanted to spend the night there so she could see how Brayden would adjust to a new crib, a new room, a new house and a new environment. I thought that it seemed like a very reasonable and mature thing to do. After all, I knew that Mollie would worry as to how Brayden was doing in a new house and what his surroundings were like.

The more I thought it over, the more I rationalized that it probably would not hurt. I did not want to bother Linda with this decision as it would have upset her, and I did not want to ruin her weekend away with her high school girlfriends. I carefully thought about it. I tried to put myself in Mollie's shoes. Wouldn't I want to know where my son was sleeping? Wouldn't I want to know what his room and crib looked like in his paternal grandparents' home? Wouldn't I want to know how he did through the night? Wouldn't I want to know how the other grandparents' house was set up? Many of these questions raced through my mind as I carefully analyzed what my decision would be.

Finally exasperated, I decided to let her go and spend the night with Brayden in his father Johnny's parents' home as long as his parents were home. I would later regret this decision as well, but at the time I thought I made the right choice.

When Linda returned from the weekend with her high school girlfriends, she was energetic and in an extremely happy mood. Weekends away with her high school friends always did this to her, and I always encouraged her to keep doing these reconnections. However, after a few days or so passed, her spirits went from a vibrant high to a sudden low. I told her about what I had decided to do with Mollie spending the night at Johnny's parents' house with Brayden. However, I did not tell her this right away when she returned home, and I should have. It actually came out a few days later as Mollie prepared for her first weekend without Brayden. She was getting everything packed in his diaper bag for the weekend at his dad's house. She was asking questions about what she should pack and then asked if it was okay if she spent the weekend there overnight with Brayden "again." Linda said, "What do you mean AGAIN?" I had not yet told her about this decision I made, and I should have. I knew that she would have rejected the idea. Maybe that is partially why I did not choose to call her and ask her opinion when Mollie had originally asked me for my permission. I do not know, but I was wrong not to tell her. True to her fine character, she held her composure with Mollie and firmly said, "No way!"

I was cringing over in our family room adjacent from our kitchen when Mollie asked this question. I knew instantly that I had committed a big error in not telling Linda. She later privately told me her feelings on this and it was not a pleasant conversation. I now look back and believe she was correct. I should have at least called her and discussed it, even if it did ruin her weekend.

Linda, as do most women, have a sixth sense or women's intuition when it comes to men or other people who are after something. She did not trust Johnny James nor his family, especially his mother, and she thought the idea was absurd. I had to ask for her forgiveness and I promised I would not make any more of these decisions without consulting her first. Time will tell if it was truly a mistake or not. The point is to let you know that these types of situations will confront you as the father of a teenager who becomes pregnant and then is an unwed mother. You must prepare to buckle your chin strap as these situations happen. With God's grace you can endure some of these mistakes you may make like I did. Try not to be too hard on yourself if you make the wrong decisions. If your heart is in the right place, you can recover from any tough decision you make. The important thing is to be honest and true to yourself while learning from any of your mistakes. Sometimes as the leader you have to take one for the team, even if it was not your fault or was unintentional.

I learned this lesson as a 17-year-old in my senior year of high school during football season. We had a very young team. We had a mere six seniors on the team and only two of us were starters. We started two seniors, fourteen juniors and four sophomores. Two people started on both offense and defense. They were a junior by the name of Tony O'Dowd and myself. We were playing an away game about an hour and fifteen minute drive west of our high school and our record up until that point of the season was a dismal 1-4. Three of the games we lost were all by a touchdown or less so we were in almost every game we played. But in one game which was the previous week we were blown out 49 -- 14. Ouch! Our coach was not accustomed to losing nor would he tolerate it if it was due to mental errors. He was a strict disciplinarian. Most of the games we lost were due to mental errors at inappropriate times in a game.

Anyway, in this particular game that we were playing it was our sixth game of the nine games on our schedule. If we lost, it would have been our coach's first season EVER as a coach with a losing record. He never told us that, but I knew because my father was his buddy since childhood and he let me know. In any event, right before halftime with the score knotted at zero -- zero, we had driven the ball from our own 24 yard line down to their 5 yard line after a completed screen pass for an apparent first down and goal to go. It appeared that we finally were going to break the tie and seize momentum of the game right before the half. However, the umpire threw a flag for an illegal lineman downfield penalty. We were penalized 15 yards and Coach Crowley was not a happy camper. We were backed up to the 35 yard line since the original line of scrimmage for the completed screen pass was the twenty yard line. Now, instead of first and goal, we faced a third down and 25 and had to get to the 10 yard line to attain a first down. On the next play, our quarterback was sacked and it was fourth-down and a country mile. We had to make up 35 yards for a first down and 45 for a touchdown. Our field-goal kicker did not have a strong enough leg to kick a 62 yard field goal, so my coach elected to go for it in throwing a pass to the corner of the end zone. The pass fell incomplete and the ball turned over on downs with less than a minute to go in the half. The other team took a knee twice and ran out the clock and soon we all found ourselves in the locker room.

When Coach Crowley finally entered the locker room, he was foaming at the mouth from anger. His eyes were bugged out and steam seemed to roll out of his nostrils as he began one of his famous halftime talks. Coach Crowley was known for turning the flow of a game around in his halftime speeches and adjustments he made to our game plans. Many times he would erroneously call out players and their mistakes to fire up the team. Unfortunately on this particular Friday night in the locker room, I was his punching bag and he lit into me as the captain and leader of our team. He screamed at the top of his lungs, "We finally managed to move the ball offensively and then that "Jackass Williams" had to go and get an illegal lineman downfield penalty!" As he shouted those words, I muttered to myself under my breath, "It wasn't me coach." Being a strict disciplinarian, he could not tolerate my insubordination and was never one to let a player's under his breath mutterings go. He proceeded to put me on the spot. He grabbed me by my face mask and shook it violently as if he was having a convulsion. He screamed to me with droplets of spit hitting me in the eye, to speak up so my teammates could hear. I told him with anger in my throat, "Coach, it wasn't me, I was not illegally downfield!"

By now Coach Crowley was furious, as I had challenged his authority in front of the whole team. He grabbed me again by the facemask and then proceeded to shake me all over the room from one end of the locker room bench to the other knocking guys over along the way all the while yelling and screaming at me. This went on for probably 15 seconds or so, but at the time it felt more like a few minutes. Fire was now in my eyes and I wanted to pulverize him. I said nothing more, bit my lip and then Coach bolted from the locker room. As the door slammed shut, my teammates saw that their captain was not immune to Coach Crowley's wrath, and that if we did not pull together in the second half, we would endure a long second half of the season together combined with an extremely long bus ride home. No one wanted to see Coach Crowley peeved because they knew what would be in store for us the next week in practice. I made a short apology speech to my teammates and said that coach was right, the penalty was called and I blew it.

We emerged from the halftime locker room humiliation determined to win the second half and the game and prove that we were winners. We went on to win the game 14 -- zero. Luckily for me, or I may have been demoted to bench warmer. That day Coach Crowley taught me an invaluable lesson. Sometimes even when it's not your fault, you have to take the bullet for the good of the team. As films proved the subsequent Monday when we watched the game film, it was in fact NOT me who had been illegally downfield. It was the guy who played offensive tackle next to me. His number was 70 and mine was double zero. The referee must have gotten our numbers confused and told my coach it was double 00, when in fact it had been number 70 who had been guilty of the transgression. This lesson helped me realize that sometimes leaders need to take the blame when it is not their fault. My coach never said another word about this incident, but it will forever be one I am grateful for.

Coincidentally, this halftime humiliation lesson taught our team how to rally together. We went on to win the last four games of the season for a winning 5 - 4 season. I was happy because I went out as a winner and would not be associated with handing Coach Crowley his first losing season. In the subsequent 1975 season, the team I left behind went undefeated and won the state championship.

The first summer of Mollie as a mom was coming to a fast close and it ended with her granting weekend overnights to her son's father Johnny. She grew tremendously as a mother and parent in that three-month period. Our family life was now closer and at a different level. We all were working hard together to make certain that both Mollie and her son Brayden could have a happy life. As a father, I was proud of her and how she handled this big adjustment. Mollie learned the art of sacrifice and how to be a leader through it all this first summer as a mom. I am confident that her future summers will be quite amazing.

*Romans Chapter 8 Verse 28*
*"We know that all things work for good for those who love God, who are called according to His purpose."*

Although Mollie's summer vacation was not really the vacation she had been accustomed to, it was nonetheless a pleasurable vacation for her and our entire family. We all grew closer together as we rallied for her and her son's future. The Lord knew what His plan was and He keeps revealing it day by day in our journey. We were shown with this first summer with Brayden that God truly helps all things work for His good when you love Him... and we do!

If you would have asked me back in the summer of 2006 when Linda and I returned from Hawaii whether I would be happy in the following summer if my teenage daughter had gotten pregnant, I am sure I would have said an absolute and emphatic NO! But now that we have lived through it, you can see how God took what Satan meant for evil, and turned it into His good. He has a purpose behind it all, and it is being revealed as each day passes. Who knows, maybe this book is part of that purpose. One thing I do know as surely as I am alive at this moment, is that He allowed this to happen because He knows that even though I am a sinner, I do love Him. He will make sure this story happens according to His purpose. For His mercy on me and my family in this trying time, I will be forever grateful.

# Chapter 10
# Her Senior Year

*John Chapter 16 Verses 20 & 23*
*"Jesus said to his disciples: "when a woman is in labor,*
*she is in aguish because her hour has arrived. But*
*when she has given birth to a child, she no longer*
*remembers the pain because of her joy that a child has*
*been born into the world."*

Thank God for our mothers and for all women. To think that after and during nine months of carrying a baby inside their wombs and feeling the pain of childbirth, they actually FORGET the pain because joy prevails. Most men I know, myself included and probably at the top of the list, would not be so forgetful. I am afraid to admit that if I was a woman, my childbirth experiences would be a one and done. I would be unable to forget the pains of childbirth and probably would spend the rest of my life whining about it.

I was able to witness the birth of each of my four children and my first grandson and in each case, Jesus' proclamation cited in John Chapter 16 above, was true. I do not know how women do it, but I believe it is part of their gifts from God. How could a pain cause joy? Since the births of my children, I have seen joy grow and multiply each day. Over the years, joy has been ever present in both my wife and my life because we got to share our lives with our children. Now that Mollie has her son Brayden, I have also seen the joy in her life. She too, as my wife Linda will attest, has forgotten what the pains of what childbirth felt like. Let me say it again one more time, "Thank God for our mothers and for all women!"

As Mollie prepared for her senior year of high school, I reflected on the differences she faced in her life in comparison to my senior year of high school. In 1975, life was much less complicated and the stresses on 17-year-olds were nowhere near what teenagers face today. Less than half of my graduating class actually went on to college since careers and jobs were abundant. You could enter a high-paying skilled or non-skilled labor job and make a very nice living and support a family without a college degree. Life was much more slow paced. We rode bicycles and if we were lucky, once in a while we could use our parents' car for a date or a night out with the fellas. Most families had one car and mom and dad shared it. The ACT and SAT college prep tests were not a competition to achieve scholarships, merely an entrance requirement.

Back in 1974 when I was going into my senior year of high school, most colleges and universities actually wanted perspective students to choose "their" school. It is not like that today. If you have over a 3.5 GPA grade point average and above a 26 on your ACT score, we will "talk" to you to see if we want you to attend our university. That is the attitude feeding today's college entrance requirements. Everything today in my opinion is almost too competitive. As a former athlete, I can appreciate competition, but I think it has gotten a little out of control and over-the-top. It puts too much pressure on teens and forces many of them into giving up on their dreams. Most of the guys I played college football with including myself would not even be accepted into the college we chose with today's academic standards.

There was pressure of alcohol back in 1974, but very little other drugs. Some high school classmates talked about marijuana, but I never saw any until I got to college. Hard-core drugs were rarely seen or heard of in my high school. A senior high school student could just be a kid and life was much simpler then. I am very thankful I was born in 1957, and would not want to be a teenager in today's competitively masked society.

Mollie had all the pressures that our teenagers of today faced plus the responsibility of a child. When I was going into my senior year back in 1974, I was worried about lifting weights and running workouts for football. Mollie was worried about changing diapers and getting a good nights rest so she could concentrate in class and graduate. Less than 30% of teenage girls who become pregnant graduate from high school. Mollie wanted desperately to be in this 30%. As far as her long range plan and college was concerned, she devised her own plan and goals without any help from anyone. Her first and primary goal was that she wanted to graduate from high school on time with her friends. Secondly, she wanted to enroll immediately into the local community college to take their nursing assistant program and become certified which was a one-year program. Once she finished that, her third goal was that she wanted to get a job in a local hospital hopefully in the one in which her son was born. Once there, her plan was to go into nursing and become a registered nurse while she works in the hospital.

Needless to say, as her father, I was pretty impressed with her plan. She developed it on her own and she owns it. When I was going into my senior year of high school, I had a much more limited plan. It was play football and hope I get a scholarship somewhere, anywhere. That was it, plain and simple. If I didn't get a scholarship, I would have had to get a factory job and earn enough money to pay for my college and take my classes at night. That was the extent of my plan.

The first semester of her senior year went very well. We continued our established routine of my caring for Brayden in the morning and taking him to our babysitter Kristen's home. Mollie continued to work after school, but only one job. She decided to quit one of the jobs since it was a babysitting job one night a week at a fitness center. She was asked by the restaurant manager where she worked to work an additional night. Linda and I continued to care for Brayden on the nights that Mollie worked. Mollie enrolled in two health occupation classes to expose her to the healthcare industry and learn preparatory activities for her chosen nursing plan.

Everything seemed to be going splendidly for Mollie and our family. Johnny James, Brayden's father had agreed to split the cost of daycare for Brayden with us. That was certainly appreciated and well received. After a couple weeks, Mollie and Johnny came up with an idea that could help me and help their son Brayden. Johnny offered to have his son stay at his parents' house with him on Tuesday evenings and all day Wednesday during Mollie's senior year. This was due to the fact that his parents were closing their furniture store on Wednesdays and they would have the time to watch him. This would also be better for Brayden, they reasoned, since he would not have to be dragged out of our house five mornings a week. This way, it would save us money in daycare, plus give us a break on Tuesday evenings. Johnny took Wednesday's off as he worked for his parent's furniture store full time and had now graduated from high school. He could watch and care for his son on Wednesdays and Brayden would further his relationship with his dad. This seemed fine to me at the time. Mollie and Johnny were still together. They came up with the plan on their own, or so we thought, and it seemed like a win for everyone.

My wife Linda, however, was very leery about this plan from the get-go. This was another time I should have trusted her mother's intuition, but I insisted to her it would all be okay. I felt strongly that we had to let Mollie make her own decisions. I would later come to regret this decision, too. Although we left all the decisions up to our daughter, we could have given her other perspectives to think about which we later learned would actually be used against her.

We had some struggles that first semester with Mollie's maternal grandfather Clarence Gates' health. He had several episodes with heart, cancer and lung problems and after several long battles, he gave up his spirit shortly before Christmas. We also began our legal struggles during this first semester of her senior year. In order for the birth cost of Brayden to be covered, we would have to become the legal guardians of Brayden. Neither Mollie nor Johnny understood the full ramifications of guardianship, so we encouraged them to speak with a lawyer. We had an acquaintance that offered to consult them for free the first time. Mollie decided to utilize this, however, Johnny at the urging of his parents decided to hire their own lawyer.

In retrospect, this was the beginning of the end for Mollie's hope to stay together with Johnny and maybe one day become a family. Trust is something that is earned not given. Johnny, for whatever reason did not trust us, which I personally had a difficult time with and could not comprehend. He felt that we were trying to take Brayden away from him and his parents. We on the other hand felt very hurt and frustrated. We were simply trying to do what was best for everyone concerned including them. If we became the guardians, then literally most all of the healthcare costs would be covered under my wife's health plan. This included the birth expenses which were large and the upcoming circumcision surgery which had to be delayed until Brayden reached six months of age. Johnny felt we were trying to take away his rights and he told us so. We assured him that this was not the case.

Johnny and his parents offered to get their own insurance to cover Johnny and his son Brayden which was also somewhat foolish and borderline ludicrous. The policy he proposed to get would be a minimal policy and cost him about $300 per month. The coverage in his proposed policy were nowhere near what Linda's policy covered. His proposed insurance policy would cover 50% of prescription costs, no well baby care, no emergency care and an 80% of costs responsibility to Johnny and Mollie until a $3000 annual family deductible was reached. We were offering to save him and his parents over $7000 per year by us taking guardianship. His proposal was not only NOT in his best interest, but also it was NOT in the best interest of his son and our daughter. Our policy had a $10 co-pay for all well baby care, it included emergency coverage, and it had no annual deductible and a $10 co-pay on each prescription. Even though our lawyer told us we could get an order that Johnny be 100% responsible for all medical costs from the date Brayden was born, we would not agree to it.

First, they were both still too young, with Mollie being 17 and Johnny 18. Neither of them could afford to be crippled with medical costs. Second, even if we had gotten a court order for Johnny to be 100% responsible for Brayden's medical costs since day one, it would not release Mollie from the responsibility as far as the healthcare providers were concerned. My older sister Liz owns a credit collection company business and she informed us of this part. Had we went with Johnny's proposed plan, any unpaid medical bills would still go on our daughter's TRW report and credit score. If Johnny refused to pay the bills, the credit collectors could and would come after Mollie regardless of the court order.

We also did not want to put Mollie in the position of having to collect the money from Johnny. If things did not work out between the two of them, and she needed $100 or more for a co-pay for a prescription or emergency care visit, she would be the one paying it and then trying to collect it from Johnny. Financially, her future could end up in chaos if we had consented to go along with Johnny and his parents' well-meaning plan. Surely they would understand this and consent to this, I thought. Well, after several meetings with attorneys, over $1500 in legal fees and the court appearances, we finally got a limited guardianship placement plan in effect. However, the battle scars of trust had laid a foundation which would later prove too immense to overcome.

Once the guardianship placement plan was in effect, we received another blow. The benefits coordinator for my wife's school called and said it was too late to go back and retroactively pay for all of Brayden's birth expenses. They had dragged the legal process on too long. This was a huge deal as it meant about $9000. Thankfully, after riding the emotional roller coaster for a couple weeks, we eventually got through this bump in the road, too. The coordinator of the benefits, it was learned, was in error and we were protected thanks to correspondence we had sent that dated back prior to the cutoff times. Thank God Linda is super organized. It was not the first nor would it be the last time her organizational skills saved our butts.

However, this unwanted and unwarranted stress further added to the mountain of misplaced trust and was not appreciated by Linda or me.

In November of her senior year, we had Brayden finally circumcised. His urologist at the hospital advised against circumcision when he was born and suggested that we wait until he was six or seven months old. He had to "grow into his penis" is what we were advised. Otherwise, if we had done it to him the day after he was born as planned, he would have trouble controlling his "urine stream" when he got older. The drawback was that he would have to be put totally under anesthetic if we waited. That was a scary proposition for Mollie and Johnny, but they still chose to wait. The surgery was performed and it was successful.

Mollie's first semester report card was once again very good. She carded two A's, three B's and a C. She accomplished this all while working four days a week in the sandwich shop, being a mom, and being a teenager. Mollie really enjoyed her health occupation classes and seemed to be very happy in her senior year. Thanksgiving came and shortly after we had to bury Mollie's maternal grandfather Clarence Gates just prior to Christmas. It was a tough holiday. He was 86 years old but had lived the past nine years in a veteran's nursing home and experienced a myriad of health problems. We no longer desired to see him suffer, but we still wanted to have him in our lives. Shortly before Christmas 2007, we were served papers of a lawsuit against Mollie by Johnny claiming paternity and a number of other claims. The papers included settlement filiations in which Mollie and Johnny would have to sign off to effectuate an agreement with a judge's seal.

Some of the things in the settlement agreement included:

- ➤ Joint physical custody
- ➤ Joint legal custody
- ➤ Keeping Tuesday overnights (even when Brayden starts school)
- ➤ Every other weekend visitations
- ➤ Only $100 per month until Brayden reached 18 in child support
- ➤ Geographic restrictions prohibiting Mollie from moving
- ➤ Shared holidays, Christmas break and three-week summer vacations
- ➤ Changing Brayden's last name to his father's last name

As a father who watched his daughter be abandoned by this young man in her junior year of high school, I was appalled and thought some of these terms were ridiculous. After treating Johnny with respect, dignity and class despite his actions, he treated us in this manner. He never even warned Mollie that this lawsuit was coming in the mail.

By the time we received these papers, we had a total of three days to read them and appear in court. I was, as you can imagine infuriated. First, why didn't Johnny tell Mollie that these papers were coming? Why didn't he share their content with Mollie? Why were we only given three days to read the complaint and agree to terms before having to appear in court? Why? Why? And Why? We had given him and his family access to see the child since the day Brayden was born despite their denial that he was the father and humiliation of a paternity test. Since Brayden was five months old, Mollie voluntarily had let Johnny have his son overnight every other weekend. No court had to be involved or papers served to get Mollie to do the

RIGHT things. She had done the right thing despite their insistence on a paternity test and allowed these visitations even though she had every right to refuse them. I truly believe looking back on it now that it was either ignorance, selfishness or a combination of both on the James family part to not realize what Mollie had done and how she had forgiven someone who questioned her integrity as a person.

In the fall of 2007, Mollie had consented to let Johnny have him on Tuesday evenings and on Wednesdays while Mollie attended and finished high school to help our family out and to further his relationship with his son. She did not have to agree to do any of this, but did it because she knew it was not only the right thing to do, it was what was in the best interest of her son. Why were these people treating Mollie this way? Didn't she deserve better treatment than this? Hadn't she been more than fair to him and his family? Many of these questions rapid-fired through my mind as I read over the papers she was served. The athletic football side of me wanted to take the young man out to the woodshed and teach him a thing or two about respect. But in the end, the Lord helped me through these feelings, too.

When someone treats you or someone you love this way, after you have been upright and above board with them, it hurts. Whatever trust had been built over the past seven or eight months with Johnny, and his family, in my mind was now gone. My respect for him as a young man and a person was now gone. But he was still Brayden's dad. What was I supposed to do? How was I to handle this debacle?

I knew what I HAD to do. Once again I had to buckle my chin strap and play the next play. Many times while playing the game I loved, things happened which broke your heart or were not fair in a game. These are

what my college coach used to call "sudden changes."
A sudden change in a football game is where character
is defined and built. A sudden change can happen
inexplicably. They imply a negative consequence or
momentum swing in a football game. If there is an
interception returned for a touchdown, an untimely
fumble, a blocked kick, a penalty killing a drive, how
will you react to these sudden changes? Coach Jim
Harkema, from Grand Valley State, taught us all that
your reaction to these sudden changes is something
you CAN control. Many times you cannot control the
sudden change. They happen in football games with
no rhyme, reason or justification just like things in
life. They happen without warning, but you can
control your reaction to the sudden change if you
realize that a sudden change is simply an opportunity
to demonstrate your character.

How was I going to react to this sudden change? Time
would tell. I knew that my football training had
prepared me in how to react to sudden changes. I also
knew that the rest of my team (Mollie and Linda) were
watching how I would react to it. Most of the people
closest to me advised me to stop all visitations and tell
them that until we are through the legal process, you
have no rights. I felt that this would be bringing us
down to their level. Ultimately, it would not be good in
the long run for Brayden or Mollie. I prayed fervently
again for God to give me His wisdom. I knew that
vengeance was the Lord's. I also knew that however
misguided and disheartening Johnny's methods were
that he did love his son. I felt bad that Johnny James
did not love my daughter the way two people should to
make the marriage that my daughter was secretly
hoping for. I could see that his love was simply for his
son and for him to be his dad. I hoped that this would
be a sign to Mollie where she would realize it on her
own.

I decided to send the document to our attorney that was familiar with the case. He looked over the settlement agreement and made some suggested corrections. I took the document and dropped it off with the handwritten corrections to Johnny's attorney immediately that same day. She was not in her office so I subsequently telephoned her and told her that we would not be attending the court hearing. I told her that my daughter was not signing this document and that we were shocked at the untimely and disrespectful way that this was handled. She chuckled and said, "Sorry, I cannot cancel the court date." I replied, "Fine, you are on your own because we aren't going." We were not showing up to agree to a document that was not in the best interest of my daughter or her son. Johnny's lawyer's appearance resembled a bulldog. She was about 5' 2" tall with short little stubby legs and a wide torso all the way up to her triple layered chin. She also had jowls that sagged over the side of her jaw line to complete her bulldog appearance. She had a way of needling me and I did not appreciate her tactics or her lack of professionalism. She said she still needed to show up for the case and file for an adjournment until a later date on both parties behalf. I told her go ahead and do as she pleased, but we were not going to be there. This too, was used against us later in court. I think it may have been part of their strategy which we later learned, but then again that would be giving her credit for being smart enough to be proactively deceptive, and I really do not believe that was the case.

The case ended up being adjourned until March 16, 2008. That gave us plenty of time to work through the issues in our mind. However, we soon learned that Johnny in fact had no real intent to come to an agreement at all. His intent was to keep delaying in writing each time we would submit a written response to his claims. He waited until February to respond in writing to our December corrections to his proposed settlement agreement. His response was one which simply muddied the water. He did not indicate whether he would agree to any of our changes or not. He merely added more ridiculous demands. It was apparent to me upon receiving this response that he was either receiving poor legal advice, or he had no real desire to work out an agreement. I would later learn that he was trying to delay past the time when Mollie would be 18 so that I could not stand up with her in front of the judge.

Each time we would confront him on talking about the lawyer's letters we received, he would say that it was his mother's idea and that he knew nothing about the letters. He would say he was okay with certain things, but then never write his approval in the letters his attorney sent to Mollie. Additionally, I thought it was part of poor advice from his attorney and his mother. I later learned that by delaying this we fell right into the hands of their well calculated plot.

Our lawyer had moved to Chicago and Johnny's lawyer knew that. He was four hours plus away in a car from Detroit and he told us that these hearings were just custody and visitation. He advised us therefore that we really would not need him anymore to represent Mollie. He said we could hire him to look at the documents and give advice, but that there was no need for him to come to court unless we wanted him there. I also thought that his honest feedback was true, and we decided not to retain him.

In our last court appearance with him, we had a hefty bill while we paid for his time to sit in court. He never said a word and we still had to pay the bill. I understood that he had to bill his time, but thought it futile to make that same mistake again.

I eventually told him that we appreciated his candor on this one and that we decided to represent Mollie ourselves. After all, I knew the Lord was going to help us. After much prayer and thought I decided to write a final letter stating that we were tired of their gamesmanship and we were ready for the judge to hear the case. I prepared for the March 18th hearing thinking the judge would want to know the entire story of what happened and that there would be some sort of testimony given. However, I learned that this was not what the judge would accept. All the judge wanted to know was whether we had reached a settlement on our own or not. When the judge learned that no settlement had been reached, she referred the case to the family counseling unit of the court. The family counseling unit is a court appointed mediation unit which tries to objectively hear the matters and make recommendations back to the judge. We knew nothing about this, but I soon learned that I had been bamboozled into this, too.

Johnny's attorney knew that once the judge appointed the family court mediation unit, he would stand an excellent chance of receiving most of his claims. She knew that by delaying long enough and making it appear that her client had been trying to work a settlement out, that the case would be referred and suddenly her client's demands had a greater chance of being agreed to. Also it would slow down again to a snails pace and extend past Mollie's 18th birthday so that she would have to stand alone in front of the judge.

The demographics of the county in which we live are from a large urban area whereby most of the cases that are referred are not fathers asking for all these privileges. Most of them are from the opposite perspective where the mothers are trying to get deadbeat fathers to pay child support and man up to being fathers. One grandfather, who was in court the day Mollie's case was referred to the family counseling unit with his daughter, came up afterwards and validated this to me. He started out and simply said, "Good luck." I thought this was rather odd and asked him, "Why are you wishing me good luck?" He warned that the mediation unit decided five years earlier with a joint custody 50/50 deal for his daughter who was in the exact same situation. He said they were still trying to fight it and that was why he was back in court today some five years later. I left the court that day feeling dejected, demoralized and played for a fool. I was not encouraged with this stranger's advice.

When it came time to speak in front of the judge that day, I told her that the counsel for Brayden's father was simply manipulating the facts and that they purposely delayed each writing of each letter for weeks after my next day written responses. I told her that his counsel implied that we did not show up in court the preceding December court date because we could not reach an agreement. I stated for the record that in fact, we only received a settlement agreement three days before we were to appear in court that previous December. Further, I lamented that with no warning from them and no time to get advice from our counsel, who had moved out of town, we had no choice but to not show up for the previous December court date. I further asked her why the law was the same for unwed mothers as it was for wedded mothers. I told the judge that I believed that each situation has different inherent rights for the father. If you are married and you get a divorce, you knowingly entered into a contract via a marriage license or a covenant with God whereby the two become one. Therefore when a divorce happens, you split anything that came about in that marriage into a 50/50 split. In my opinion, that includes children. However, when unwed mothers have children, there was never a legal contract nor a covenant with the father, so technically the mothers and fathers rights should not be treated the same as those who were married. The judge agreed with me in concept but said, "Unfortunately Mr. Williams that is not the law." We were referred to the family mediation and counseling unit.

The family counseling unit was a group of master degreed and PHD social workers who would interview the parents of the child as well as the grandparents. Neither party's lawyers could be present which I found odd. The counseling unit itself was located in a building straight out of the 1930s. The building was built in 1921 and was about 15 stories high. Its decor was dark and dingy and gave me a bad aura. So much so, that I could not sit still while in the waiting room of the counseling unit.

That early spring morning as Mollie, Linda, Brayden and I entered the family counseling unit building, I felt anxious, but knew we were well-prepared. I had advised Mollie that this was probably going to be the most important sales call of her life. In an hour or two, she would have to convince the assigned mediator that she was a great mother who had always done everything in the best interest of her child. I had learned that once these cases are referred to the family counseling unit, there were 12 factors that the counselor/mediator would evaluate in making their decisions. It seemed very odd to me that someone could make an assessment like this in just an hour or so interview. Mollie and I put together a 15 page PowerPoint presentation on these 12 factors in order to give the counselor our feedback on each of the 12 factors. Some of the factors included, the moral fitness of each parent, the ability of each parent to give love and affection, the ability of each parent to provide food, clothing and shelter, the ability of each parent to foster a relationship with the other parent and whether or not each parent had a criminal history that would place the child in danger.

As we entered the Family Court entrance on the seventh floor, we were greeted by a friendly security guard who told us that our cell phones were not permitted in their unit. The counseling unit consisted of a very small reception area with a long dark and dreary corridor with offices on each side. There was a large waiting room in one of the offices. Linda, Mollie and Brayden headed over to this reception area as I scurried down the elevator to put all three of our cell phones back into my car. The car was parked in an outdoor parking lot about three blocks from the counseling unit building. By the time I made it back to the building, Johnny James and his parents had arrived. Mollie, Johnny and Brayden had already been called into the counselor's office and were nowhere in sight.

The waiting room was cold and filled with tension. As I entered, I was greeted with a look of indifference as my wife rolled her eyes. Johnny's parents were sitting directly across from her and the wall of disdain was so incredibly high I could actually feel it. After 15 minutes or so, Johnny came out of the counselor's room with Brayden in his arms and gave him to his parents. By that time, I had already gotten up and walked to the corridor several times back and forth pacing like a nervous caged animal. I preferred to stand so I could observe the tension. Neither of us spoke to each other, nor said hello. We refused to acknowledge each other's presence, which was fine by me. As far as I was concerned, they were invisible not even there in the same room. I had made my mind up that I was not going to talk any longer with either Brayden's paternal grandparents or his father. Their behavior had sown the seeds of mistrust and malcontent. Mollie and our family had trusted them and for our trust, we were rewarded or shall I say were betrayed with repeated episodes of dishonor. I knew I had to forgive them, but it does not make it easy. If they apologized and asked for heartfelt forgiveness, it would be much easier.

As soon as Johnny came out of the counselor's room, he turned and went back into it with Mollie still there. I studied Brayden from the rear of the room where he could not see me and saw how his other grandparents interacted with him. He obviously was loved by them and you could see that. As he went back and forth with books and toys between his two grandmothers, I had to leave the room. This was more than I could take. The poor little guy had no clue that his two sets of grandparents did not care for each other and it was a foreshadowing of what his future may be like. Innocently, he loves both sets of his grandparents but practically it will be a difficult life for him. I decided to go and tell Linda that I could no longer wait in the same room with these people. It was time for me to leave and roam the building. I promptly proceeded to roam the halls for the next three hours and 15 minutes. The counselor it seems was having a marathon session with Mollie and Johnny. As I paced and walked the building floors, I prayed out loud in chants and in repetitive fashion "Lord Jesus please bless Mollie with your wisdom and grace." It was probably the longest three hours of my life. When my wife Linda finally came to find me in one of the hallways, we were asked to come in and speak with the counselor. It was just Linda and myself in there and I pondered on how this session was going to go. I had wondered if Mollie was going to show the PowerPoint presentation to the counselor while Johnny was there. I did not know that she had requested the last 15 minutes with the counselor alone without Johnny present.

As we entered the counselor's office, I was still somewhat nervous and so was Linda. The counselor was a bright and cheery African-American lady about 45 years of age. She asked us to sit down and she proceeded to tell us how impressed she was with our daughter and her accomplishments of not missing any high school and being just one month shy from graduation. She said it was rare for her to see this and it told her that she must have come from a good family who provided a lot of support. She proceeded to tell us that she was concerned about the father's inability to listen and the fact that he did not tell her the truth about his most recent drug charge. On March 18, 2008, Johnny had been arrested for drug possession and when asked about his drug usage, he did not mention it. This was a huge concern for her as well as us. Neither she nor I wanted our grandson to be around anyone who uses illegal drugs. The fact that he told her he was convicted in 2006 for marijuana possession and had finished a year's probation made himself look cleaned up.

But when she asked him when the last time he used drugs was, he shrugged his shoulders and told her he could not remember. She told us that it was then in front of Mollie where she had a red flag go up. Normally if you quit doing drugs due to a conviction and probation, you would know the date or approximate month you quit. The fact that he said he could not remember posed a serious red flag. She went on to tell us that Mollie had requested the last 15 minutes alone with her because she wanted to show her the PowerPoint presentation. When she saw a copy of his most recent March 18 offense and arrest which was in the power-point, she was even more concerned. She told us that normally in a case like this, she would recommend a 50/50 split with joint physical and joint legal custody. However, she was concerned about him not acknowledging the most recent charge himself when she had given him the opportunity by asking pointed and direct questions. I told her that I was concerned for my grandson's safety and my daughter's future. I told her that according to the State of Michigan Custody Guidelines Manual that if joint physical custody was awarded, that my daughter would be sentenced to living the next 17 years in her current town. This is because the Custody Guidelines Manual clearly said she would need either a court order or Brayden's father's signed consent that she could move anywhere. I told her that I was 100% sure that he would never consent to her moving and that it was an unfair financial burden. I asked her for mercy upon my daughter. She indicated that was not her understanding of joint physical custody. I told her that I would send her a copy of the subsection I had read it in. It was clearly written right in the Michigan Child Custody Act Manual.

As we prepared to leave her office, she turned and abruptly asked me her final question. "Do you think Johnny is a good father?" Startled I looked over to my wife, and asked her if she would like to answer this first. Linda said, "No you go first." I started out very cautiously! I knew I had to be honest, but I also had to relay my concern. I said that I had no doubt he loves his son, but that a father had to show his love for his son by setting a good example. He needs to have character and make good decisions. I told her that he has the potential to be a good father, but that his actions concern me. First, he would not admit that he was the father and he yielded to his mother's demand for the paternity test. Then, he abandoned and ignored my daughter while she endured her pregnancy journey alone at 16 in her junior year of a large suburban high school. Third, he had no plan for his life with college or formal secondary schooling. Fourth, he uses illegal drugs and I did not want our grandson in a situation where he could be hurt due to his dad being stoned or on drugs. Finally, I told her that all through the legal process he repeatedly surprised my daughter with ridiculous letters from his attorney. Character is what you do when nobody is watching. I told her that character is what defines you in times of adversity and that I did not like the character I was seeing in him as a person much less as a father. My wife Linda echoed my sentiments. We shook hands and left her office.

In Mollie's second semester of her senior year, she did have a lot of fun times. She played on a powder puff football team. She still had occasional sleepovers with her best friends and she went on a spring break trip.

Linda and I had debated agonizingly about the spring break trip very seriously for several weeks. We had consented to spring break trips for Mollie's older siblings, so we felt we should do the same for her. All of her older siblings' trips were chaperoned by other parents, while we paid for the trips. It was their high school graduation present, from mom and dad. This time though, our daughter had a son and a responsibility she would be leaving behind. If we allowed her to go, what message would we be sending? If we told her to stay home and be a mom, then how would that directive be perceived? Either choice we made came with consequences. Linda and I discussed this at length and eventually decided to let her go to Florida as long as mom and two of Mollie's friends' mothers could go and chaperone. Mollie would have to ask Johnny if he could stay home that week to watch Brayden.  Mollie was very happy with this and willingly made all the arrangements.

Two weeks before she was to fly to Marco Island, Florida with my wife Linda and her friends for her senior spring trip, she was called by Johnny and learned that he had decided not to watch Brayden that week. He was offered a chance to go to Myrtle Beach for that same week that she was going to go on her Spring Break trip. Once again this was another case where he showed his level of maturity and character. Now the only way that Mollie and her friends could go on their spring trip was if she could find a substitute babysitter. As Mollie contemplated the few choices she had, it was obvious what I needed to do. I decided to take a week of my vacation and watch Brayden for their trip to Florida. I get 28 days of vacation and usually lose 7 to 14 days a year. It was a no-brainer for me. I had a great time that week watching him knowing that my daughter got a break like all of her older siblings did.

Mollie and her friends together with the moms, had a riot on their spring break trip. I was told the moms actually had more fun than their daughters, if you can believe that.

Brayden and I also had a great time while his mom and grandma were gone on spring break. We went swimming twice to an indoor pool, read books, took stroller rides in the local indoor shopping malls, and ate our meals together. We even attended church together.

The one thing that we did that contributed to Johnny's malcontent was we both got our haircuts together one day. It was a spur of the moment decision. After a stroller ride in the mall one day, I decided to get my haircut since in the forthcoming week, I was going to be packed with important meetings. I wanted to look good, so I knew I had to get a haircut. Once I got there, I decided to cut Brayden's hair too, which was his first haircut.

I had not even thought about it being a problem nor did I think it would be negatively received. A very kind lady at the barbershop took pictures with a disposable camera which she had in her car. She overheard me telling my barber that it was Brayden's first haircut and I was grandpa. She graciously offered to be the photographer and I accepted. I offered to pay her for it, but she declined. She said if it was the first haircut, then I should take pictures so I would not get in trouble with Brayden's mom. I knew Mollie would be fine with it, but I did not anticipate Johnny's negative reaction to it. I got the pictures developed afterwards and gave both Mollie and Johnny a picture and lock of his hair. Mollie thought he was cool and had no problems whatsoever. Johnny initially seemed okay with it, when I presented the lock of hair and pictures to him in my home when he returned from his ten day trip. He thanked me and went home. He had come over to see Brayden when he returned from his trip to Myrtle Beach.

A few minutes after he drove home, our telephone rang. His mother got me on the phone and reamed me out with a few expletives. I held my cool and simply told her that she was entitled to her opinion and I was entitled to mine. Obviously, we disagree and I told her that I would have to hang up now. She actually beat me to the hang up. For her to insult me and disrespect me for giving Brayden a haircut seemed like another slap in the face that was uncalled for. She would have to realize that her son and my daughter were not married and these are part of the consequences he would have to deal with. It was only a haircut for crying out loud. As Mollie maturely pointed out, "Dad, Johnny could take him for his next haircut and take pictures for his scrapbook then. Brayden would never know the difference."

I guess this is what you can expect from a family that raised their only child to live on peanut butter and jelly sandwiches (with the crusts cut off) and Pringles potato chips. Yes that is correct, Johnny only eats peanut butter and jelly and Pringles with Coke for every meal. Breakfast, lunch and dinner consists of P&J, Pringles and coke. Weird diet huh? Poor guy is missing a lot.

When Mollie told us of Johnny's diet and lack thereof, we believed she was fabricating it as some sort of joke. However, after repeated attempts to have him eat breakfast, lunch and dinner at our home or when we invited him to come out and eat with us at a restaurant, we learned that this was the case. His diet was P. & J., Pringles and coke. Occasionally, he will eat chocolate pudding. Thank God Brayden eats most everything you present him and does not have this eating disorder.

Once Mollie returned from her spring break, she focused on completing her last eight weeks of classes and graduating. She finished the second semester of her senior year with a 3.0 GPA securing two A's, 2 B's and 2 C's. She also had enrolled in Schoolcraft Community College and was accepted into the nurse's assistant program. She started classes in July and will complete the degree within a year. When her June 15th graduation day came, I was very proud to see her walk up the aisle with over 600 classmates and receive her high school diploma. She had accomplished a very important step toward the execution of her plan. She had made it into the less than 30% club which meant she was ahead of most of her peer teenage pregnant counterparts.

There were a lot of people who gave her help along the way; her teachers were fantastic. Her counselor Mrs. Brunch was absolutely phenomenal. Her babysitter Kristen will forever have a place in my heart for helping Mollie and our family. She surely would not have been able to do it without her. Her friends

Morgan, Natalie and Samantha were always there for her. A lot of our family and close friends helped along the way, too. Her girlfriends took turns occasionally babysitting when Mollie had to work or study for tests.

As she walked up to receive her high school diploma, I sat there with my wife Linda, my dad, his wife Rose, my son Steven and his girlfriend Katie and I had a huge lump in my throat. I knew that together, Linda, Mollie and I with the Lord, had buckled our chin straps in order to help this goal be realized for Mollie. The Lord's help was abundant and I only hope one day Mollie will reflect on this chapter of her life and realize that this help came from Him in the form of His people who loved her.

*First Peter Chapter 1 Verse 6 & 7*
*"In this you rejoice, although now for a little while you may have to suffer through various trials, so that the genuineness of your faith, more precious than gold that is perishable even though tested by fire, may prove to be for praise, glory and honor at the revelation of Jesus Christ."*

At the start of this chapter the verse I used from John chapter 16 spoke of a woman's anguish being replaced by joy. This verse above in First Peter spoke not only of the anguish referred to by John but tells us we should rejoice in our sufferings and trials. Once again how can a person rejoice in suffering and trials? Can you rejoice in a trial?

Each of us endures trials as we journey through our earthly lives. I truly doubt that we rejoice in them. That is our Lord's challenge and also His promise. He promises us that the trials will only come for a little while and that if you place your trust in Him, He can help you get through them.

The challenge that my daughter faced as a 16 year old being pregnant was indeed a trial. It did cause our family suffering and yes, we were in anguish. But joy has returned and we now rejoice. Our daughter has graduated from high school. We have a grandson. Our lives are different than we had planned them to be, but our faith remains genuine. This book in some small way may help to prove that human trials endured can be used for the praise, the honor and glory of Jesus Christ.

In football, when your helmet gets knocked off, you buckle your chin strap and play the next play. In life when the sufferings and trials come, you must buckle your chin strap too, and play the next play. If you buckle your chin strap with the Lord though, He will help pull you through your adversity and trial. The glory will be His, but the blessing will be yours. Joy will come. Rejoicing is possible. Buckle your chin strap and you will see.

# Chapter 11
## And Lightning Strikes

*Jeremiah Chapter 20 Verse 11*
*"But the Lord is with me, like a mighty champion. My*
*persecutors will stumble, they will not triumph. In their*
*failure they will be put to utter shame, to lasting*
*unforgettable confusion."*

Who is the greatest defender of all time? What sport did he or she play? What are his or her records? These questions are often debated when it comes to basketball, hockey, football or soccer and other sports. A myriad of many names of famous athletes surface when trying to name the greatest defender of all time. But none of them can compare to the Holy Spirit. The Holy Spirit is the greatest defender of all time. He helps His servants and was promised to us by Jesus Himself to defend us in our battles.

I have always known that the Lord's Holy Spirit has been my greatest defender. Twice when I was growing up, I nearly died from accidents. Once when I was in fourth grade, I nearly fell into a sewer with a manhole cover off. The second time was in a swimming pool accident in sixth grade where I almost drowned. In each case it was as if an outside force lifted me from the danger to safety. It may sound freaky, inexplicable and odd, but while hanging on for dear life as a young child around 9 or 10 and screaming from the edge of a sewer hole, I was suddenly lifted to safety by a guy who seemed to appear out of nowhere and then just as suddenly, he disappeared. Then in my swimming catastrophe, I tried to dive off a diving board and kept sinking while swallowing water each time I came up for air in a junior high school swimming pool. I pulled two of my friends in who tried to save me and suddenly a huge force propelled me up and over the side edge of the pool. As a child I never really thought much of it, but I have never liked sewers or water since. In fact up until now, I have never told anyone about these two experiences in my life! I think my defender wanted me to live longer and so He sent His angels to help me in both those experiences.

On June 30, 2008, we were scheduled to go back to court and appear before the judge to settle the custody and visitation matters between Mollie and Johnny James. We had been anxiously awaiting the report from the family counseling unit. The counselor told us in our visit with her in May, that we should receive the report at least a week before the court date. Therefore, we expected to receive the report by Friday, June 27th at the latest. Each day that week when the morning mail came, we hurriedly sorted through the stack of letters and bills to see if the report was there. On Thursday the 26th, my daughter Mollie decided to call the counselor herself and left a message but "still no report." When the mail came on Friday, we learned that the report was still missing in action (MIA). Mollie decided to call the counselor again and fortunately she was able to reach her this time. The counselor said she would have the report in the judge's hands by Monday and Mollie could get a copy then.

By now as you can imagine, we were frustrated and disappointed. The court had required us to prepay for the report and the family counseling court fees in advance. However, we would not know the results of the report until standing before a judge. This seemed totally unfair.

This could have forced us to make a premature decision. I was concerned that our attorney was no longer retained and that we would go into court and be forced to make a premature decision without the time to think through all the ramifications. I also was not sure if I would be allowed to speak as a representation counsel for Mollie.

As I prepared for Mollie's high school graduation party that Friday afternoon, suddenly the telephone started ringing. We had decided to give her a graduation party the last weekend of June, so both Linda and I were scurrying to and fro like busy elves getting ready for the next day's party at our home. Each time the phone rang, it was Johnny James' lawyer. She, too, was concerned that there was no report. Mollie was at work so she could not talk with JJ's lawyer. She asked if I thought Mollie would agree to the original settlement paperwork that she sent to Mollie way back in December with all of my handwritten corrections. Stunned I told her yes I thought so, but why the sudden change in heart? She stated that if we went to court with our own agreement, already agreed to, it would not matter what the report said. I wondered, "Why then did we just go through a long delay and have to pay family counseling court fees if this was agreeable?" It made little or no sense to me. She went on to say she would only be adding a few changes to the agreement. I told her that I had to see the changes in writing before we would agree to them. She assured me that the changes would only be minor and clarification terms. I went on to tell her, that with all due respect, she represents her client and that if there were changes of any kind, I needed to see them. Furthermore, I would have to see at this late juncture if I could get in touch with my lawyer who now has moved to Chicago. As we continued the telephone conversation, I abruptly pronounced that I did not trust her, nor did I respect her. I was trying to get my tent up for a graduation party the next day and here she was at 2:15 p.m. on a Friday afternoon trying to badger me into agreeing to something. It did not feel right.

Johnny's attorney seemed annoyed and preoccupied almost like she was in a big hurry. She hurriedly said she would not make any of the changes to the draft agreement which she had referred to because it was too late in the day. It was now almost 2:30 p.m. on Friday and she had a 3 p.m. court date. I knew at this point that I was being lied to, as I deal with District Courts in my job and no court hearings start on a Friday afternoon at 3 p.m. So, I decided to play along with her game. I exclaimed, "Wow, that is not my problem," I told her. "But rather, yours and you can work on the retyping of the changes tonight after your court." I knew she was lying to me and by this point in time, you could hear the frustration in her voice. I finished by saying, "Please e-mail the document with the changes typed tonight to me." At this point, she became annoyed and she got extremely flustered. She said, "I have commitments tonight and all day Saturday and Sunday. I cannot type these changes by then." I knew she could handwrite them and have her clerk do it if it was important enough to her, and I could not stand being lied to and manipulated. Never trust another party's lawyer. EVER!

Once again, this was another warning signal. This lady was not only unprofessional, but she was a pathetic liar, too. I told her that I regretted that she had other commitments, but that I would still need to see the changes in writing. If I could not see the changes in advance, then I told her we would have no deal. I needed to see any changes in writing. I felt it was reasonable to want to see these changes in writing prior to the Monday court date. I even suggested that she pay her clerk or secretary overtime to type all of the changes.

By now, she vehemently disagreed and told me she was going to call her client back. She said that she would see if he would accept the original changes I made back in December to her settlement proposal, with none of her new changes/clarifications since she did not have time to type them. "Accept the original agreement without her clarifications that had seemed so important back months ago?" I questioned. By now she really had me wondering what they were up to. Magically, she called back 10 minutes later and said she talked with her client, and "they" had said "they" would agree to the December document with all my changes and no further changes. I told her we had a deal and that I would see her Monday in court. But I silently wondered why she had said "they" and not "he". I believe she had called Johnny's mother, not her son. "His mother must be worried about something," I thought. I went on to finish setting up for Mollie's graduation party which went splendidly by the way.

Then later that night a freak of nature occurred or what some may call an "Act of God." Lightning struck the court building in downtown Detroit where we were supposed to appear in court that following Monday. The building caught fire and suffered considerable damage. They had to postpone all court cases while the building repairs and fire remediation and restoration work was done. Was this fire an accident or an act of God? I thought it was the latter. For some reason, the Lord did not want us to go to court that Monday. I knew in my heart that my defender was once again defending us to make sure that His justice was served.

We had learned from the counselor that she could not cite Johnny James as guilty of his most recent drug possession charge because he had not pled nor was he found guilty of the offense. Johnny we learned had hired a high-priced lawyer in town that was his next door neighbor in this criminal case which we found very peculiar. This lawyer was running for district judge and knew all the judges and court personnel including the prosecutor. He was supposed to have a pretrial hearing and plead on June 2, 2008. But his lawyer got it postponed for six weeks until July 15, 2008. They wanted to plead after Mollie's and Johnny's court appearance for the custody of Brayden so that it would not jeopardize the court's decision with regard to custody, visitations, etc. I felt that this was devious and showed once again the character of the people who were Brayden's other family (his father and paternal grandparents). Could it be that the Lord struck the building with lightning so that he would have to plead before our case was heard? Did the Lord want us to see a copy of the court appointed family counselor's report before we went to court? I felt in my heart at the time that this was not a mere coincidence. It was my defender once again playing great defense.

However, when Johnny's July 15th rescheduled appearance date for his criminal case came, he once again tried to slither away and hide behind a rock. His lawyer filed a new motion for another six week extension. Our court case for Brayden's custody had not yet been rescheduled due to the fire, but they were obviously buying for time. Each time Johnny went to court for his criminal case, we hired a private investigator to go and observe the court proceedings. This way we would know what was going on with his drug possession charges. I did not really have a fear of going to those proceedings myself, but we did have a fear as to how Johnny might react to our daughter Mollie or their son. We felt it would be best to discover and learn covertly through a private eye. Our daughter's life was already going to be tough enough with this guy and his parents. Why add fuel to their fire, we reasoned.

Finally, three days before the last day of July, my wife decided to call the court to find out when our custody settlement hearing would be rescheduled. To our dismay, the court clerk announced that it had already been rescheduled for July 30th, 2008. That was only three days away and we had not received a notice in the mail or even a phone call. Typical of the court system, it is slow, bureaucratic and ineffective. In hindsight I think to this day, that the court had told Johnny's attorney what the date was, but she purposely did not share it with us. By now both parties had finally received a copy of the family mediation counselor's report. Upon review of it, they saw as did we that the Family Counseling Unit's recommendations were actually better for Johnny, than what we had negotiated and agreed to over the telephone when Johnny's attorney had called me frantically that Friday in June. This was while I was getting ready for Mollie's graduation party. The counselors report recommended sole physical custody and joint legal custody with three weeks summer vacation and shared holidays. Many of the other items we had verbally agreed to were not in her report. Johnny and his lawyer saw this as an opportunity to get more than they had agreed to in our last phone discussion. Little did we know that they secretly planned to have amnesia and pounce on Mollie in a couple days on the July 30th, 2008 court appearance.

When we arrived at court that morning it was a beautiful summer morning. The sun was shining and the humidity was low. The birds were singing and all seemed quite nice. However, I did not have a good feeling as we walked to the courthouse that morning from the parking lot some three blocks away. I felt that something was not right and I could not quite put my finger on what it was. I soon found out why.

As we rode the elevator up to the court, the four of us, Linda, Mollie, and Mollie's older sister Amber who had returned home from Florida, all joined hands and prayed for God's wisdom and His justice to be done. When the elevator doors opened, we were greeted by Johnny's attorney. We were 20 minutes early and it was obvious she had been there for a while. That immediately struck me as odd since, she had done everything else to that point at the last minute. She told us that they had decided to adopt the family mediation counselor's report and that our agreement was no longer going to be honored. This infuriated me. She and her client now had a case of serious amnesia and were going back on their word via our telephone agreement. I did not let her see my frustration as I simply said, "Okay." I knew then, that we were in trouble. I figured that if she was going back on their word for the oral contract we entered into, she knew something that I didn't know. I would soon learn a lesson that was painful and very frustrating.

The judge was a little late that morning in starting. We were supposed to start court at 9:00 a.m., but it did not begin until around 9:20 a.m. When she entered the courtroom, all had to rise and then our case was the first one she called. As she announced Johnny James versus Mollie Williams we all rose and proceeded to walk to the judge's bench. This time as I walked to the bench, the court officer, a big burly Italian looking man with big brown round eyes and a round belly stood up and approached me. He asked, "Are you her lawyer?" I remarked, "No I am her father but I am representing her." He said, "You are not allowed to be up here with her, you need to go sit down." I firmly said, "Wait a minute sir, I was allowed to represent her last time I was here, why can't I be up here?" He could see I was frustrated and mad, but told me sternly, "You need to go and sit down NOW!" Now I saw why Johnny's lawyer had amnesia. It was becoming painfully obvious why she had arrived early to the courtroom that day. She had talked to the judge and court officer and told them that Mollie would not be having a lawyer with her and that as an adult now being 18 years of age, her father was not allowed to represent her unless I had a law license which I did not. In our previous appearance before this same judge, Mollie was only 17 and I had embarrassed Johnny's lawyer and called her out with her deceitful manipulation of the facts in how she had previously communicated them to the judge. Johnny's lawyer knew that Mollie would not have our lawyer there to represent her because I had told her that I was not paying for him to drive all the way back from Chicago (that was another big mistake I made). "Besides," I reasoned to myself, "We didn't need him there since we had already verbally agreed to the settlement she drafted and I corrected way back in December of 2007." Now she was going to pounce on my daughter and she did so like a ravenous lion. Johnny's attorney knew Mollie's personality and that she would be docile and scared out of her mind. She knew that Mollie would just answer the questions. Mollie was meek and although she will inherit the earth, she would not be very assertive in this environment. Things were looking really bleak.

Johnny's lawyer proceeded to go on offense attacking Mollie with a number of claims and statements. She opened up by stating that her client would accept the Family Mediation Unit Counselor's recommendations, but that she was filing an order to allow Brayden to travel to North Carolina for a family vacation for 10 days. She went on once again to twist the facts to say that Mollie knew about this vacation and had previously been invited to attend, but now had decided not to go. She was painting a bad picture of Mollie going back on her word, and I wanted to jump and scream that she was once again lying and twisting the facts. As I sat there in the courtroom I was squirming in my seat in frustration, rage and anger. She told the judge that Brayden was going to go on the airplane without his father and with his paternal grandmother. The judge asked Mollie if this was true. Mollie was so nervous I could actually see her knees shaking. She told the judge she knew about the vacation, but was not comfortable with Brayden going on an airplane without his mother or father. Then Johnny's lawyer jumped in and said that Johnny was driving down there to save money on airfare. The judge thought that Mollie might be able to pay half of Johnny's airfare which was absolutely ridiculous! At $4 a gallon for gasoline, it would cost over $300 to drive there and back. I was getting more and more frustrated as I felt betrayed, lied to, cheated and physically charged up.

By this point in the whole charade, I wanted to throw some forearm shivers to this lady's head. I wished I could strap on the leather, and shoulder pads and deliver pancake hits to this amnesia laden lawyer, the partial judge, the egotistical court officer and mostly to Johnny's mother who I believed had orchestrated this whole deception ordeal. The judge said that this decision for travel to North Carolina was up to Mollie, but asked her if she was in agreement with the Family Mediation Counselor's recommendation. She said, "Yes for the most part." Then the judge asked her what part did she not agree with. Mollie indicated that she did not like that he got Tuesday's overnight when Brayden starts school and felt it best for him to be in his own home every school night. The judge appreciated this, but swept it under the rug by saying, "You can come back to court and get that changed, there is plenty of time left before he will start school since he is only a year and half old." We wanted all these things in writing to protect Mollie financially from having to go back to court every time and pay additional court and attorney fees which we had funded thus far. Then the judge went on to tell Mollie she needed to give a copy of the birth certificate to them if she agreed to let them fly. She ordered Johnny's attorney to draft a settlement filiation awarding custody and other matters.

Then she adjourned our case pounding her gavel. It was my second experience in a courtroom in my life where false witness was given against me although it was really on my daughter. If I had been allowed to speak, I would have put that attorney on defense and turned the tables. We had an oral contract which I had brought a copy to show. She had agreed approximately 30 days earlier to this contract in our telephone conversation. I knew that an oral contract was binding just as a written one was if acted upon. I could have crushed her if given the chance. I was fuming.

As I got up to leave the court, I felt like I had been railroaded and worse yet, I had not protected my daughter very well. I should've hired a new attorney and had him there so that he could go on offense with Johnny and his attorney. I felt that my defender had let me down, but I also learned a valuable lesson. The only winners in a court of law and a custody case are the lawyers and the court system. The system is set up to keep the lawyers in business. The lawyers, if they are good and politically astute, will someday become judges. Then when the judges have their re-election campaigns who do you think will attend their fundraiser parties? That's right, you guessed it, the lawyers do. It is a big you feed me, I feed you game.

As I walked out of the courtroom with my tail between my legs, once again humbled, I had been asking the Lord, "Why would You let this happen to my daughter? How could You abandon me and my daughter and let this injustice stand?" It occurred to me some weeks later though, that maybe He did answer our prayers and He really made sure the best thing for Brayden had happened. Maybe I did not like the end result, and how the proceedings were conducted, but in reality the thing I was most fearful of "joint physical custody" did not happen. Mollie would still have sole physical custody and as such, she would have the freedom to move anywhere within 100 miles without having to go back to court and/or get permission from Johnny. I had prayed for the Lord to give us His wisdom and justice prior to exiting the elevator that morning and maybe justice was still being served. Time would only tell.

As I exited the courtroom, the burly Italian looking officer who had ordered me to sit down, requested that I meet him in the hall in five minutes. He could see that we were frustrated and I think he truly felt sorry for our daughter Mollie and the way Johnny's attorney treated her. He told us that he had been doing this job for 24 years and that whenever one party shows up with a lawyer and the other one does not, the person with the lawyer always wins. He told Mollie that she would most likely be back in this same court room several more times over her son's life and asked her if she had a lawyer. Mollie said, "My lawyer moved to Chicago." He said, well I am not really allowed to tell you this so I will turn and tell the wall instead. He then turned to face the wall and said, "I know a really good lawyer by the name of Tim Dunnigan who has a really good reputation with this judge and her court. I could totally understand why you may want to contact him. His office is in Westland, Michigan on Warren Road." I told him, "The wall had a hard time hearing the lawyer's name and address so could you repeat that for the wall?" We got a pen out of my wife's purse and wrote this lawyer's name and address down for later use. This officer's kindness illustrated to me that there still are good people left in the criminal justice system. Not all of them have lost their integrity. It is not right that you have to hire a lawyer to receive justice, but I would never go to court again without an attorney.

As I reflected later that day, I thought about the girls who could not afford attorneys and may have found themselves where Mollie was today. What about all these poor teenage girls who get pregnant? What do they do when these legal things happen to them? How can they afford attorneys? Mollie was actually lucky she still had us to help her. These questions are still very troubling to me. The girls who become pregnant as teenagers need advocates and they need help so situations like these can be averted. Hopefully, this book can help.

The legal struggles we experienced with guardianship, custody/visitation, and the friend of the court matters are part of the consequences fathers of teenage girls who become pregnant need to be cognizant of. If your daughter chooses to keep her baby, and you support her, you will need to buckle your chin strap and get ready for some big hits. As a former football player or athlete you will have the attitude that you must win at all costs just like a football game. However, the stakes are much higher in this life changing event. Don't focus on winning as much as what is in the best interest of your grandchild and your daughter. Sometimes you may get lucky and the father and his family would not put up a fight. You must be ready for the fight though. Don't fight the fight without a lawyer. Get the best one you can afford. If you could avoid the fight by getting the father to sign away his rights early on in the pregnancy do that. It will be difficult to do this if the father is less than 17 years of age. Your daughter as mine did, still may have the dream that she and the baby's father can be, "one happy family."

That was the paradox my wife and I struggled with throughout this journey.

When Johnny abandoned my daughter at 16 and immediately got another girlfriend, I should have moved in and tried to get him to sign off his rights. Most likely he would've done that, but I did not want to hurt my daughter and her dreams of being one happy family. It was a tough call. I did the best I could. That is all any of us fathers can do. If you do your best and ask God for His guidance, and trust in His outcomes, then you have done all you can do.

I also learned that you should never talk to the father's lawyer. They will use your innocence against you as all they are about is winning for their client. If you don't have a lawyer, don't speak with the father's lawyer. If you can't afford a lawyer, see if you can get a pro life or churchgoing lawyer to donate his or her time to help you. It is my hope that one day the law will change so that teenage girls who become pregnant are given there inherent rights back. The teenage unwed mothers should always receive the sole physical custody of the child unless she is mentally, emotionally, or physically unfit to have possession of the child. If the mother has a criminal record or is involved with drugs and addictions, then these factors should be considered as well. It's not good for any child to be around illegal drugs or criminal activity. Secondly, I firmly believe that the teenage unwed mother should be allowed to move anywhere in our country where she chooses without petitioning the court or the father. That way if she can move to obtain a better paying job or if her future husband gets transferred, she would have the inherent right to do this. After all, the teenage girl was the one who had morning sickness, and/or the rumor mill at high school, saw her body go through all the physical changes and experienced the pains of labor and birth, NOT the father.

There was no binding legal contract between the teenage mother and the father in the form of a marriage license, so the court should not penalize these teenage girls. Their lives are going to be tough enough. By limiting their ability to move, the court handcuffs the teenage mother and sentences her to a life of a criminal. It is as if the teenage mother is tethered to live in her locale for the next 18 years and I believe it is not morally or legally right to do this to our daughters. The teenage mother did not commit a crime. She made a poor choice and a poor decision as did the teenage father. Most of the consequences of the event are all on the mother and her family. The father should have rights, but not the same rights of children born from a legal marriage or union. The father's inherent rights should be joint legal custody for health and welfare and every other weekend visits along with summer visits. I believe this without hesitation and bias because I could have a son be on the opposite side of this issue and would still feel the same way. I can honestly say that if my son had fathered a child out of wedlock as a teen, I would still say that the mother should have those rights. It is unfair for the law to apply mothers and father's rights equally as there is a legal line of demarcation since they are unwed.

The profits, if any, of this book will be used to set up a foundation to help support poor teenage pregnant mothers. Some of the help I hope to give is help for counseling, education including college scholarships, day care assistance, diapers, clothing, shelter, job training and legal representation. Most teenage girls who become pregnant are not fortunate enough to have a mother and father who will help them. Often they are from single-parent homes where they are struggling financially and lack the ability to sustain a family for their child. The result is a vicious cycle of poverty that sentences the mother and her child to a lifetime of misery. It does not have to be this way though. Things can be different. The keys are education, faith and support. The foundation will be set up with those pillars. The education pillar will focus on helping the mother complete her high school degree, college or trade training and/or job training for career development and placement. The second pillar of faith will help the mothers find friendship and advocates in faith-based organizations and churches. The final pillar is Support which will be supporting the teenage mother emotionally with counseling if necessary; financially with food, clothing, diapers and living expenses; and spiritually with Christian Fellowship in nurturing.

*Matthew Chapter 15 Verse 11*
*"It is not what enters one's mouth that defiles that person; but what comes out of the mouth is what defiles one."*

Now that time has passed, I can see why God really had a lightning bolt strike the court building and delay the settlement custody hearing. He wanted to teach me the lesson spoke in Matthew about keeping my tongue on guard for the sake of His justice with our grandson. Being a football player, your natural instinct is to retaliate when you are being attacked. In a court setting things may come out of your mouth that defiles not only yourself, but your God. That is part of the lesson I learned. Another one of the most difficult challenges we faced was to guard your tongue when you are being persecuted, tormented or attacked by your grandson's father's parents and his legal representation. But for the sake of my grandson and my Lord, He taught me once again to guard my tongue. It was only through God's tremendous grace that I kept my tongue silent and still when in front of my adversaries. I will let vengeance if any be the Lord's. I am determined with His continued help to remain stoic and stand with my tongue on guard. Through His grace neither my wife nor I will ever say a harsh word about Brayden's father or his paternal grandparents. His life will already be difficult enough. I will continue to pray for strength each day to keep my tongue on guard so that I defile neither my God nor myself. By staying in control of my tongue I have taught God's lesson not only to my daughter, wife and grandson, but hopefully to Brayden's father and his family as well.

# Chapter 12
# 55 Yards to Texas
# College and Beyond

*Matthew Chapter 6 Verses 19 & 21*
*"Do not store up for yourselves treasures on earth,*
*where moth and decay destroy, and thieves break in*
*and steal. But store up treasures in heaven, where*
*neither moth nor decay destroys, nor thieves break in*
*and steal. For where your treasure is, there also will*
*your heart be."*

As you journey through your life, where will you store up your treasure? Will you work to acquire wealthy possessions and things? Or will you work to help others, create eternal friendships and live God's gospel? These verses really spoke to me as I confronted my daughter's teenage pregnancy. What was the Lord telling me to do? I think He was telling me not to worry about using the wages I had been blessed with from my job to spend on my enjoyment and retire early as I had planned. I have always been a goal oriented person and had the goal to retire by 55. I did not want to retire to stop work; I just wanted to retire to find an area of my life where I could do something that truly could help others. I want to do something that makes a difference for our Lord, before my time here on earth is finished. These verses challenged me to think of where and why I was going to store up treasures that I earn from my job. If I buckled my chin strap, I could keep working and apply the treasure to help my daughter and my grandson.

The moment I reflected on these verses, I knew that the Lord was telling me to keep working and stop worrying about storing up my treasures. He wanted me to help my daughter and my grandson. He also told me that by writing this book, I might be able to use any of the treasures from book sales to help all of HIS other daughters who are poor and need help as they confront their teenage pregnancy. With God's mercy and grace, my treasure is now being focused on helping my daughter and all daughters along with their fathers/mothers with this book. I am certain that when I die and go to heaven my treasure will be stored in the souls of those whose lives I have helped even if it only ends up being my daughter and grandson. I sincerely believe that the memories we share and the lives that we touch here on earth cannot decay, nor can a thief steal them. They will last throughout eternity and through God's grace they will be multiplied one hundred fold throughout the generations.

On December 6, 1978, my teammates and I persevered through a pounding rainstorm and a foot and a half of red clay in a mud-box that was our national semi-final football game field. My GVSU offensive teammates and I huddled for what was to be the last drive to those of us who were seniors' football careers. The All-American center I played next to for all four years, Bob Beaudrie, told everyone as we got into the huddle, "Only 55 yards to Texas boys!" The winners of this game would enjoy a trip to McAllen, Texas, where the National Championship game was to be played. We had possession of the ball on our own 45 yard line after our defense forced an errant 6 yard punt off the side of their punter's foot. We were down by a score of 13-7, but we still had over four minutes left on the clock to score a touchdown and an extra point to win the game. I don't think there was a guy in that huddle who believed we would not succeed. We knew we were the better team and we knew we could score as long as we took care of the football with no turnovers. It was paramount that each of us did our jobs. We believed we would certainly score. I remember buckling my chin strap extra tight as we gathered in the huddle for the last drive to glory.

Everything seemed to be going according to the script. We proceeded to drive the ball down to the 14 yard line with relative ease and precision despite the rain, mud and deplorable field conditions. Virtually every play we ran was a running play and we were dominating the line of scrimmage. There was still over a minute left and we had a first down but no time outs left. Our coach decided to stop running the ball and elected to throw after the first down play that netted only a two yard gain. Our quarterback killed the clock with a pass out of bounds on the next play. We still had 2 downs and 47 seconds on the clock left to get either 8 yards for a first down, or 12 yards to score the winning touchdown. However, with no time outs left, it was a little dicey to try and run the ball. So Coach dialed up his pass plays. We threw the next pass to the corner at the end zone and it fell incomplete just over the receiver's outstretched hands. Now there were 39 seconds left with one final down. As I lived through the awesome experience, I remember asking the Lord to help us score and do our best. We had all worked so hard and I felt we deserved it. However, other teams practice, too. Their players work hard, too. They have guys who pray and probably were praying that day, too. So in the end, I knew I just needed to do my job and let the chips fall where they will.

As we prepared for the fourth down play, I wondered if it would be my last. I thought of all the years I had played this wonderful game called football. It had been fun and I had learned a lot about myself and how to persevere through things that happen. It was an excellent training ground for another game called life. I had 100 percent confidence that we would score and that we were going to win the game. Our coach called another pass play which gave our quarterback three options. He would roll out to the right on boot leg action and he could run if it was open, throw to the tight end in the back of the end zone, or throw to the flanker who was running a crossing pattern over the middle. It was a great call. We had scored on this play many times during the season. As we broke the huddle, we all stormed to the line of scrimmage and got ready for what was sure to be a touchdown. Our quarterback rolled out and sold the run well enough to leave our tight end open in the end zone. He made a valiant pass in the back of the corner of the end zone to our freshman fourth string tight end Rob Rubick. Rob had it in his hands for a second, but as he was falling to the ground, he was hit by an Elon College defensive back and the ball fell incomplete. Rob felt terrible but went on to set all types of receiving records for a tight end at GVSU. After graduating he played for the Detroit Lions in the NFL for five years.

As the ball fell, so did our dreams of a national championship and a trip to McAllen, Texas, where the championship game was played the subsequent week. It was a huge disappointment to everyone on our team. Four years of hard work, effort, and dreams came down to one final play. A pass play with rain still pounding us and our uniforms so soaked and drenched with the rich red clay soil of North Carolina, that you could not even read our numbers or team name. Each of us felt that if we had played the other team on a dry field, we would've won. But the 55 yards to Texas came up 12 yards too short. Our season was over. For those of us who were seniors, our playing careers on the gridiron had to come to a disappointing, rain soaked and frustrating end. As I walked off the field for the last time, I was struck by the irony of my last game played in the mud. When I was a child growing up, I loved to play in the mud. My mother would constantly yell at me for tracking it into our house or for getting my clothes ruined. I had to chuckle to myself as I left the field muddy from head to toe. As I walked my way over to the end zone where my parents waited to see my brother and me, I laughed to myself, even though I was disappointed. My mother greeted me and said, "Now do you know why I always have told you that nothing good can come out of mud?"

Mollie now has a similar situation with her life. Her goal is not a national championship. Her goal is to attend college and get the nurse's assistant one year degree. After that, she plans to find a job in a hospital and pursue getting her Registered Nursing degree which is a four year degree. She too, is 55 yards from her Texas. Undoubtedly, she too, will run into obstacles. The obstacles won't be the red North Carolina mud and rain, but rather financial struggles, time for her son, legal matters, custody matters, and parental philosophy barriers. Some of these I can help her with, but some of these she will have to conquer on her own with God's help. Her task will be to put forth her maximum effort to achieve her goals, knowing that along the way there will surely be obstacles. Hopefully, she will "Buckle Her Chin Strap" and play each play one play at a time. If she does, I feel confident that her life will be fulfilled.

Our college coach, Jim Harkema, had a saying about effort. He believed that there was no such thing as 110%. He believed that all you can give toward an objective or a goal is 100% or the "maximum effort." How can you give more than one hundred percent? When you really think about it, one hundred percent is the maximum; it is everything that is possible. If you give your maximum effort, you can achieve your goals most of the time. Sometimes you can give a maximum effort and still fall short of achieving your goal and that is okay. The important thing is to give your maximum effort. Then if you fall short of your goal, at least you know you gave it all that you had.

Our team gave a maximum effort my senior year in the 1978 Mud Bowl to try and get the opportunity to play for the first program national championship in the college's history. It was not the most talented team I played on, in my five seasons at Grand Valley State. But it was the team with the most heart. Each player gave their maximum effort and as a team, we did reach our potential. Even though we were disappointed for not accomplishing our goal, we knew we left it all on the field. We had no regrets.

This is so true with anything in life that matters to you. If you give it your maximum effort and fail, then you have nothing to be ashamed of. It could be your marriage, fighting a disease or addiction, your job, your children, your coaching, your hobby, your aging parents, or your pregnant teenage daughter. All you can do is give your maximum effort. You may not get the entire result that you desire, but in the end you can rest assured that you gave it your all. You gave it your maximum effort!

In my years of coaching my children in sports such as baseball, basketball and soccer, I received many reminders of Coach Harkema's lesson on maximum effort. I tried to teach it to the children I coached. Sometimes we won games we had no business winning, while other times we got beat in lopsided non-scoring affairs. There were many soccer games that I coached where we had no business even playing as we were far out matched in abilities and/or talent, that we managed to squeak out 0-0 ties because the kids gave it their maximum effort. If asked to choose between a player with talent and one that played with maximum effort, I would always rather take the kid who gives it his or her maximum effort all the time. When someone gives it their maximum effort, they have the chance to fulfill their potential in whatever endeavor they are working for.

As a coach, I tried to teach that winning was important but not as important as giving your maximum effort. I stressed team over individuals and drilled the players on repeated fundamentals every practice that I could. I had two experiences that I will never forget. One coaching experience was in the sport of basketball and the other one in soccer. As a coach, I always wanted the children to experience what it was like to score, get a hit or make a basket. Many kids can play an entire youth soccer career, for example, of five years or more, and never score a goal. My objective was to give each child the opportunity to score in each season. I did like them to experience what it was like to win, but it was not my primary emphasis. I always gave each child the opportunity to be in a position where they could score the goal.

One season in indoor soccer, I had a chance for everyone to score in the season as long as "Raven" our defensive fullback in outdoor soccer, could score in our last game. Raven was probably 10 or 11 years old at the time, and she was one of the more serious girls on the team who always gave her maximum effort. She had never scored a goal in all her years of soccer up to that point since her previous coaches always put her on defense. As we started that last game, even though we were undefeated, I told the team that our objective was not to win; it was to get the ball to Raven when she was in so she could score a goal. I told them that if she scored, it would be the first time in all my years of coaching that every single player had scored a goal in a current season. Fortunately, girls understand better at that age than boys. Boys at that age want to score and win and that is their focus. The girls wanted desperately to help Raven score and knew that winning was not the only thing. The girls did an awesome job and gave Raven at least a dozen chances to score. Each time her shots would either be stopped by the goalie or sailed just wide or north of the goal. You could see that all the girls were trying to help Raven score a goal. I was very proud of this group of girls for trying to execute passes to Raven throughout the entire game.

Finally, I took Raven out with just over four minutes to go in the game still without her scoring a goal. I told her to get a quick drink and that I was going to put her right back into the game. Before she went out, she knew I was a Christian and I told her I was going to bless her and say a quick prayer. I blessed her with the sign of the cross on her back and asked the Lord to help her launch the ball into the goal. Raven sprinted back out to the field and within less than a minute she drilled a low shot into the corner of the goal. The parents in the crowd and her teammates went crazy. It was a time where maximum effort was rewarded and everyone on the team scored a goal that season. We ended up winning that game which was a bonus and the team went undefeated for that particular season. It was the only team I coached in soccer where everyone scored a goal in that particular season. In the fourteen years I coached soccer, no other team even came close to this accomplishment.

In another sport, basketball, I had a very similar situation occur. Bobby a hard worker but slow feet and not a very athletic young man was on my sixth grade Catholic Youth Organization (CYO) basketball team. He was the only one who had not scored that season and it was our last game. The week before the game, my assistant coach Jim Brennan and I came up with a double screen play that we could run in order to give Bobby an uncontested shot and a chance to score in the game. We worked on the play all week in practice. When game time came, I gave a similar speech to the boys and we had a similar result. Bobby actually scored five points that game! Two buckets on the uncontested double screen play and he made a free throw on a foul shot. The parents in the crowd went crazy when he scored also. Both Bobby and Raven were not very athletic children. They were heavier than most of the children on the teams that I coached, and were not blessed with an abundance of speed or athleticism. Both of them were excellent listeners and both of them strived to do their best at all times. They always gave me their maximum effort which is really all a coach can expect out of any player. Neither child ever missed a practice. Neither child ever disrupted practice or antagonized a fellow teammate. They were both really good kids who deserved a chance to score and feel what it was like to be a star. In each case, their scores brought tears to my eyes and prayers of thanksgiving to the Lord. I was absolutely thrilled to see their accomplishments! Also, in both of these games, their teammates were thrilled too, which made their accomplishments even sweeter to me. In each game, not only did each player score for the first time of their lives, but the team saw the value of working hard for someone else to help them achieve their goal. The winning was always secondary to me in youth sports. I left each contest with goose bumps down my spine and a coach's grin from ear to ear.

I picked these two highlights from my coaching days to illustrate the importance each father has in the role of helping his teenage daughter should she become pregnant. She will need a coach who believes in her and someone who will put her in a position to score. I tried to do that with Bobby and Raven and in each case, they produced the desired and expected result.

They knew that I personally believed in them. Now my daughter needed me to put her in a position to score. She would need my help financially, emotionally and spiritually. She also knew that I believed in her. She has had 18 years now of my telling her that I believe in her and also showing her with my actions that I loved her.

Would I have liked Mollie to finish high school, go to college, get a job, meet a great guy, get married and THEN have her first baby? Heck yes, but life does not always work that way. Many of the plans you make in life get detours or roadblocks. However, I could still show my daughter that I believed in her. She could still reach her goals and potential as a person, a mother and a nurse. That will be my job now as she pursues her college years and beyond. I pray that God will let me live long enough to see His plan come into fruition.

My prayer for Mollie and all teenage pregnant girls who choose life and/or keep their child is that they can have a father or mother, or both, who will believe in them and help them. Someone who will give them their opportunity to be fifty five yards from Texas, too. If not a father or mother, then maybe someone such as an aunt, an uncle, grandparents or an older sibling that could be there for them. Teenage unwed mothers need to know that someone believes in them and loves them. They need to be put in positions to score and feel like a star even if it means sacrificing something for the greater good.

*Luke Chapter 9 Verses 23 & 24*
*"If anyone wishes to come after me, he must deny himself and take up his cross daily and follow me. For whoever wishes to save his life will lose it, but whoever loses his life for my sake will save it."*

I believe that these two verses above, in Luke, are the BILLBOARD verses for true Christians. In your lifetime you will be constantly confronted with challenges, storms, roadblocks, disappointments and disasters that will define how much you truly believe in your faith. When these events come, will you try to save your life or will you lose your life? Will you buckle your chin strap with the Lord or will you take the easy way out? My friend, the only choice I believe that you will find ultimate happiness with when the challenge comes, is to lose your life. If you try to save your life, in the end you will lose it. By losing your life as you may have planned or wanted, you will actually gain it and much more.

Our daughter became pregnant at the tender age of 16. She chose to lose her life, not save it. She chose to give her baby life, not kill it. She chose to stay home to attend college, not go away like her brother, sister and friends. She chose the hard road, not the easy road. She is losing her life as society defines it for the normal teenager, but in the process of losing her life, she will actually save it. She could have been irresponsible and selfish and yielded to what society says is merely a choice. In her heart she knew that it was much more than a choice. It was a life. By losing her life as she knew it, I believe she will actually save it.

Mollie's decision to lose her life would not have been possible if my wife and I had not decided in our own way to lose our lives. We could have told her she had to get an abortion. We could have kicked her out of the house as many weak and ill informed parents do. We could have told her that she had to give the baby up for adoption. We didn't, we left the decision up to her and told her we would stand by her and help no matter what she chose. We are fortunate in that the Lord has blessed us with the means to help our daughter and our grandson. Some parents may not be in a financial position to do that and choose adoption which is also a responsible choice.

Both my wife and I were seeing the light at the end of the tunnel in terms of raising our children. Mollie was our last child and all the others were either graduated from college or in their final two years of their college studies. Now we have elected to take a detour. Our home is once again turned into a nursery with toys, diapers, and baby bottles all over. We will not be spending our time for just us as we had planned now. We will be spending time with our daughter and grandson helping them. But in the end, by sacrificing to help our daughter and her son, we will receive much more. This teenage pregnancy event has helped and will continue to help our marital love keep growing, prospering, and flourishing. It is not easy and at times has been exhausting, but it will be worth it. Linda and I will continue to give it our maximum effort and "Buckle Our Chin Straps" with the Lord to help Mollie and Brayden's lives be fulfilled in college and beyond.

# Chapter 13
## Too Young to Die

*Romans Chapter 14 Verse 7 & 8*
*"None of us lives for oneself, and no one dies for oneself. For if we live we live for the Lord, and if we die, we die for the Lord, so then, whether we live or die, we are the Lord's."*

As I prepared to write this book I debated on whether this chapter should be the beginning or the end. I figured at first since this was really the beginning of the story, I should start with it. But the more I reflected and prayed about it, I felt sure that this should be the end. Hopefully you will understand why.

On March 24, 1988, the beginning of this book was being written, although at the time, I really was oblivious to it. I was on top of the world. I had been blessed with a newborn son who we named Michael that weighed 10 lbs. 2 oz. on this day. Michael Richard Williams was added to my two and a half year old son Steven and my five year old daughter Amber. My job was going great and I could not have been any happier with my life. My wife Linda and I were content in our marriage and our family at that point in time was now complete. Linda had some difficult pregnancies and after having the last two babies by cesarean section, the doctors advised us to tie her tubes. I will never forget this day. The day our son Michael was born. The sun shined brightly and it was a crisp spring morning the day Michael was born. The grass had just started to turn green and some of the buds on the trees were already blooming. The birds were singing a marvelous tune and it was a perfect morning. As we drove to the hospital together that morning, Linda reminded me of our first trip there when Amber my oldest was born. She had actually gone into labor a month before the due date and we were scared to death as we drove to the hospital. Her water had broken and she did not even have her bag packed. On that morning back in November of 1982, I made sure I stopped at every stop sign and even stopped for the yellow traffic lights. Linda was upset with me and had told me to just run the light and the stop signs since she was scared. Today our drive was much more relaxing and we actually reflected on all of our drives to the hospital together when our own miracle of life(s) were born.

Soon after a reflective and relaxing drive, we arrived at Butterworth Hospital in Grand Rapids, Michigan. Linda was promptly wheeled from the admitting office into the surgery room since it was another planned cesarean section. I met her there after parking the car and changing into my surgical scrubs. The same butterflies I mentioned earlier were there and within no time Michael was pulled out of Linda's womb. He was not crying and was extremely alert and I remember that he just kept looking at his mom. As Dr. Van Dommelen asked me if I was sure we wanted to tie Linda's tubes after Michael was cleaned up from the cesarean section, my heart was in my throat. I gazed into my wife Linda's bright blue eyes which were still soaked with tears of joy and it was as if the room around me was spinning while my heart thumped in drum-like fashion in my throat. When I saw her nod yes, with tears in our eyes, I simply told him, "Yes." I saw him cut her fallopian tubes with his scissors and then cauterize them. Afterwards he proceeded to stitch her up while Michael still lay on Linda's chest. He was making little gurgling noises and sounded like a pigeon with his little coos.

We had spoken to our pastor about the tying of her tubes and whether we should do it or not. He had advised us that it was our decision to make, not his. He said that since Linda was so small and our babies were so large, God would understand. All of our children except Amber had been born from C-sections which were considered dangerous to a woman's health back in 1988. We made the decision to tie her tubes and went forward.

When we brought Michael home, our house went from busy to chaotic, but in a good sort of way. Steven and Amber adored their little brother and were eager to feed him and take turns holding him. After six weeks maternity leave, Linda had to go back to work. She really enjoyed the time with Michael and his brother and sister, but she needed to get some rest and go back to work. For any mothers out there who have had three or more children under the age of five, you know that it is a lot of work to watch over this many young children without an adult to talk with.

We were very lucky to have an awesome angel of mercy by the name of Audrey Ulanowicz to baby-sit our children. Audrey attended our church which was called Church of the Holy Spirit and came highly recommended. She did not baby-sit for the money. She did it for the love of children. She had been our sitter for almost five years since Amber was born. We felt especially blessed to have her in our lives and her husband Carl, too. There were as many as seven children at her house, but most days only four or five children. All of her own children were grown and out on their own.

We had debated on whether or not Linda should realistically even return to her job. With three kids and paying a babysitter, we wondered if it was financially worth it. We figured that in another year our oldest child Amber would be in school full-time and then we would be back to two kids at the sitters so we decided we could try it for a year. We also knew how much our children loved Audrey and their friends who also were cared for at Audrey's house. I saw firsthand that Linda loved staying home with the kids, but I also knew that she was a busy body who loved to be on the go and to talk with people. After much soul searching, we thought it was a good idea for her to try going back to work for a year and see financially if it was worth it even though Audrey's babysitting would take most of her check.

Linda's job did not start until 9:00 a.m., so she always got the kids ready and took them to Audrey's house each morning. I did the easy part and picked them up each day around 5:30 p.m. I really did not appreciate how difficult it was on Linda until I had to get my grandson Brayden ready every morning. I learned just how much work it is to get one child much less three of them ready to go to the sitters early in the morning. I now appreciate my wife even more! I only had one to get ready with Brayden. Linda did all three of our children every morning. She must have been totally exhausted by the time she got to work each day. How she did it with three kids I will never know. Thank God for Linda!

In no time, the ten weeks for maternity leave had vanished, (six of the weeks paid and four of them unpaid) and it was time for Linda to return back to work. It was very difficult for her to leave Michael with Audrey, but the fact that Amber and Steven were there that first Monday, June 6, 1988, made it easier. Linda left them all at Audrey's home and I picked them up at the end of the day. Everything went splendid that first day back at "the grind."

However, the next three days would be a difficult test. On Tuesday morning, I had to travel down to Cleveland, Ohio, for our mid-year review meeting which would last three days. I would be back by 8:00 p.m. Thursday night as long as traffic was smooth on the ride back home. I remember feeling guilty leaving Linda that Tuesday morning, with three kids and a job, trying to do everything. However, I had no choice. The meeting was mandatory and I was up for a promotion, so I could not jeopardize that. "If I got the promotion," I thought, "Maybe we could afford to have Linda quit and stay home with our children."

As I drove to Cleveland that morning, I reflected on how blessed I was to have a beautiful wife who is also my best friend and three beautiful, healthy children to share my life with. The meeting started at 9:00 a.m., so I had to leave my house by 5:30 a.m. in order to arrive on time.

The first day of the meeting went fine. We covered the usual topics such as where we are today in orders and where we needed to be by year end. Action plans were discussed to get us there. That evening the regional sales manager took us all out to an exclusive restaurant for a really fabulous meal, but I could not eat. I had felt sick to my stomach for some unknown reason. Maybe it was the drive, lack of sleep or just plain worrying about Linda with all three kids and no help. I left the restaurant early after picking at my steak, and retired back to my room. Once I got to the room, I promptly called Linda on the telephone from the room to see how it was going. It was still early around 9:30 p.m. The kids had just gone down for bed and she sounded very tired. We talked for a while just small talk, and finally we both decided to hang up and go to bed. That night at about 3:00 a.m., I woke up suddenly and startled in the dark hotel room. I was drenched in a cold damp sweat and I was literally sitting up on the edge of the king-sized bed with my arms outstretched and lunging forward. I was reaching for something or someone, but I could not visualize what or who it was. It was a very confusing and troubling moment. I immediately got up went to the bathroom, and changed my T-shirt which was soaking wet with the perspiration. I hung the wet tee shirt on the shower curtain and then drank a cold glass of hotel water.

I returned to the bed intent on revisiting my slumber. However, try as I may, I could not get back to sleep. I tossed and turned and the vision of me reaching for something kept playing back and forth in my head. What was it? Who was it? Why was I reaching? None of this made any sense. I tried to turn on the TV and get something else into my brain, but still no sleep could be found. Finally, at about 4:00 a.m., I decided to get up and go out for an eight mile run. I was big into long distance running and had begun training for my first marathon. By the time I got outside for the run it was about 4:15 a.m. and still dark outside. I was wide awake and felt the run might bring some clarity to the dream I had just awakened from.

I finished the run about 5:30 a.m. and did some cool down stretching in front of a packed hotel parking lot for another ten minutes or so. Once my body cooled down, I returned to my room to get cleaned up and get ready for our second day of meetings.

Our regional sales manager had made it his practice for each sales rep to give a presentation of their current sales results and their plan to make and exceed their personal plan. I had to look over my presentation notes and prepare for the day. After showering, I ordered coffee and oatmeal in the room through room service and I began studying my materials. I had about an hour or so to study since the meeting started at 8:00 a.m. In the back of my mind though, the dream I had was still haunting me. It was a struggle to concentrate much less finish my oatmeal. At approximately 7:50 a.m., I left my room and made my way down in the rickety old elevator to the large foyer where our meeting was being held.

Our regional sales manager finished his "Winning Way" presentation to the group of over 40 sales people right around 10:00 a.m. The "Winning Way" was a sales qualification tool which helped us qualify a sales opportunity. It dealt with whether the sales opportunity was worth it, was it real, could we win and what was our strategy to win. It was very interesting and the time seemed to fly by. I actually forgot all about the troublesome dream I had the night before.

Once he finished his presentation, it was our turn to start our individual mid-year results presentations. We had to give our presentations to our colleagues so it could be a little nerve wracking. Our Regional Manager Rip Jackson then asked for volunteers and when no one volunteered, he decided to go in alphabetical order. Rip was an African American long-time 30 plus year manager in our company and had been my personal favorite corporate leader in the company over the years that he managed. I would run through a brick wall for that man. He eventually took an early buyout and retired to become a Christian minister in his church in Arizona.

As I sat there listening to my colleagues the rest of the morning, my mind kept flashing back to my dream. I reasoned that it must've had something to do with my anxiety over the presentation which I had to make in front of my peers. I was comfortable making presentations in one-on-one customer meetings or small groups, but I secretly dreaded presenting to my peers. I think most people fear presenting in front of a group of their colleagues more than they do any other group.

As the morning passed, I regretted not volunteering to go first as we were only halfway through the presentations and it was shortly before lunchtime. I knew that I would be second to the last since my last name began with a W. The anxiety of waiting was now bothering me. To this day I do not know why I did this, but as the regional sales manager announced that there was time for one more presentation before lunch, I raised my hand and asked if I could go. I was tired of the anxiety of waiting and felt it best to just get it over with. So Rip reluctantly let me go next.

As Rip was introducing me to my peers, suddenly the foyer door swung open and there was a bellman who rushed into our meeting room with a slip of paper in his hand. He handed the slip of paper to Rip who was standing in the front of the room with the microphone introducing me. After reading the slip of paper, he handed it over immediately to me with an inquisitive and worried look on his face. He said simply, "This is for you." As I read the note, my face turned completely white and my legs went limp. My troubling dream suddenly crystallized before my eyes as I read the note. It said: emergency for Dick Williams call Audrey!

As I read the note, my mind flashed instantly back to the dream. I remember thinking at that moment, "There is no way Audrey would be calling me unless something serious, something very serious had happened." I knew instantly that someone close to me had died and was being taken from me. My arms had been outstretched in the dream because I was reaching for that someone who was being taken from me. However, I could not remember the face or who it was, but my mind knew from the dream that someone was gone.

After reading the startling slip of paper, I told Rip and my peers that I had to be excused since there was an emergency at home. As I raced to the nearest pay phone, my heart pounded like a bass drum, and I prayed frantically to my Lord. "Please dear Jesus, please help me with this phone call. Please do not let my dream come true." Back in 1988, cell phones were a luxury and expensive. They had just started entering the market and we were not permitted to use them. We had a 1-800 calling card and I rapid fired it from memory into the nearest pay phone. As I dialed the number, my heart was now in my throat and suddenly I heard Audrey's voice. She was still in shock and robotically answered my questions. The conversation went something like this:

**Audrey:** Hello.
**Dick:** Audrey this is Dick. What is wrong?
**Audrey:** Michael has stopped breathing and is in the hospital please come home.
**Dick:** Audrey, please tell me, is he still alive?
**Audrey:** He has stopped breathing and is in the hospital please come home.
**Dick:** Okay Audrey, what hospital?
**Audrey:** Butterworth Hospital.
**Dick:** Where is Linda?
**Audrey:** At the hospital, please hurry home!
**Dick:** I'll be there in three hours. Bye Audrey.

As I hung up the telephone, I ran to the bathroom and started uncontrollably vomiting. My stomach was now united together with my heart inside of my throat. I knew that Michael had died even though Audrey would not tell me on the telephone. I had been warned by the Holy Spirit in the dream. I felt helpless and terrified. I needed to be there quickly with my wife

Linda and children. Now I had to drive home and I would not be able to drive my car home fast enough. But first I would have to go in and tell Rip and my sales colleagues that I had to leave.

As I frantically re-entered the ballroom foyer meeting room, you could hear a pin drop. I told everyone that I had to leave immediately because my infant son had stopped breathing. I promptly turned and left the room. Before I could get too far, Rip caught me and insisted that I fly back home. But I tried to be stubborn and told him, "Don't worry Rip I will be alright, I will just drive my car back, thanks though!" That way I thought, "At least I would not have to come back down to Cleveland to get my car next week." Rip would not accept no as an answer. He promptly drove me to the airport and put me on the next plane to Grand Rapids, Michigan. A few days later he drove my car back to the office from Cleveland and I picked it up.

As I flew home that day, I clung to the improbable hope that Michael was still alive, but down deep inside my soul, I knew he had already gone home. My dream had told me so. When I stepped off the plane my first boss from the company I have worked at now for 28 years greeted me. He told me what I already knew, that Michael had suddenly and inexplicably, died. He drove me to the hospital where I eventually found my devastated wife Linda. Needless to say she was delirious with sadness and pain and so was I. How could he die so young? Of all our children, he was the only one to receive a 10 on his Apgar score, which is a ranking system from 1 to 10 on an infant's health. Why did this happen to us? We were a good Catholic, Christian family. Why was God allowing this to happen? Poor Michael "Spike" as I called him, he only got just under three months to live. This was not fair.

What was I going to do now? I wanted to crawl into a hole and die.

The next several days were a blur, but the Lord did bring us through them. The funeral home was packed on both nights of the visitation/wake and hundreds of people came. We felt so blessed to have so much support in our time of grief. Michael's funeral mass was beautiful as difficult as it was. For years after his death, I was troubled that he did not go to heaven. It turned out that the day we buried him was the day he was scheduled to have been baptized. Finally, after talking to a priest years later and listening to Catholic Answers a radio program, I found peace. Michael is in heaven due to baptism by desire. We had desired to get him baptized and in fact had it scheduled for the day he went home to see our Lord. Michael Richard Williams only lived 3 months and went to his eternal home to live with Jesus on June 8, 1988. I had a difficult time imagining heaven without my children there with me, so this was a welcome realization. Thank you Jesus!

We discovered a week or so after Michael's funeral that he had died from SIDS which is an acronym for Sudden Infant Death Syndrome. It is a terrible disease that has happened to families since the early days of civilization, where the infant, usually between three and nine months old, inexplicably stops breathing and dies. There have been several studies conducted and theories as to the nature of its cause, but no one knows definitively what the underlying cause is of SIDS. Hopefully some day they will find the answers.

Two weeks after Michael died, I was offered the promotion I had worked for and coveted. But it no longer seemed appealing. I was down in the dumps and very depressed as I grieved and longed for my son, Michael. I would never be able to throw a football with him. I would never be able to take him golfing. I would never be able to play baseball with him. It was for me personally the MOST trying time in my life.

I was being transferred from the Grand Rapids, Michigan, branch to the Detroit branch as the branch sales manager, which was three hours away on the east side of the state. The timing could not have been worse, from the standpoint of relocation. How could I move my wife and children 160 miles away from all of their support and help while we were still in the grief process? Was I being selfish? What kind of a husband and father was I? I almost called Rip and told him that I could not take the job since the timing was not right. However, as I thought and prayed about it, it was almost as if God wanted to give us a new start. We decided to take the promotion and soon I was off to Detroit commuting for the first 60 days until I could find a new house. My company would purchase my old house if I was unable to sell it, but it sold in a week.

I subsequently read somewhere that over 75% of the SIDS marriages unfortunately end in divorce. Also of the remaining 25% of the SIDS marriages that last, over 95% of them end up moving out of their home. As it turned out, despite the difficulty and timing, our move to Detroit did happen to be one of the better things that happened to us while struggling in this life defining event. It was extremely difficult to enter Michael's bedroom for everyone in our family and especially Linda. Although Michael died in Audrey's home, it was still very hard to live in the home that he had brightened so beautifully even if it was only for three months. We sure missed him.

We learned some years later that the coroner and police had wanted to do the autopsy. We did too, only so we would know if there was something we needed to worry about in our two living children Amber and Steven, so we gave them our permission to conduct the autopsy. The police we learned had treated our Audrey as some sort of criminal as if she had murdered Michael. They did an investigation at the scene and hammered Audrey with all sorts of criminal type questions. I know they were just trying to do their job, but they had no idea of who Audrey was. She was a model caregiver. Audrey tried to apologize several years later at her daughter's wedding because the police and coroner's office had made her feel guilty. Linda and I were literally devastated when she shared the news to us on how the police had treated her this way. We did not learn of their treatment of her in this manner until several years later, otherwise I would have personally called the officers and their superiors and read them the riot act.

I found it extremely difficult to accept an apology from someone who had nothing to apologize for. Audrey had nothing to be sorry for and we still loved her like a big sister. But that night at her daughter's wedding, I could see that Michael's death was still eating away at Audrey. She had been storing up the remorse and guilt from the manner in which the police treated her and she needed desperately to know that she was forgiven.

I knew by telling her that she was forgiven, even though she had nothing to be forgiven of, that she would be able to put it behind her (hopefully). Let me tell each of you that although we keep in limited touch with Audrey and Carl since our move, they are two of the dearest friends and caring angels that God has sent into my life. I do not know why God chose to take Michael away in Audrey's house. It was not fair for her to endure the years of guilt she has carried. We told her she was forgiven, shed a few more tears and enjoyed the rest of her daughter's wedding reception, as best we could.

I will never forget what Audrey told me a few days after the funeral. She told me that when Michael died, "He had a big smile on his face." She said it was because, "He has a secret." I asked her what the secret was and she told me that when we go to heaven one day, we will find it out. I think Audrey was chosen as God's instrument of love to not only help Linda and me and our family as a caregiver, but as Michael's human bridge to his secret. For that I would be eternally grateful to Audrey. She was chosen by God for this task and as difficult as it has been on her, she performed her mission with wonderful grace and mercy. She was a blessing to us and Michael.

Our move to metropolitan Detroit was shocking. The prices for homes were more than double what we had sold our Grand Rapids home for and everywhere we looked, we found sticker shock. It seemed like we were going to go backwards not forwards with our standard of living. We hired a real estate agent who took us to homes in at least six different communities. Every home that was in our price range either needed a lot of work and improvements or was located in an area that did not meet our standards. Depressed and downhearted one night while swimming in the hotel pool where we were staying, a young lady overheard us talking about our inability to find an affordable house. She told us we should look in a community called Plymouth/Canton. She said that they had good schools and you could get a lot of house for your money. She was right. We checked it out the next day and purchased a new home in Canton, Michigan, where we still reside today.

That autumn, after much prayer and long discussions, my wife Linda and I made the critical decision which was one of the best decisions of our married life together. We had decided that God may want us to restore her fallopian tubes with a re-tubaligation surgery. This is a surgery where a surgeon through microsurgery reconnects the tubes which were cut, cauterized and tied preventing fertilization of eggs. The surgery would cost about $7,000 and was an elective surgery which meant it was not covered by our medical insurance.

I remember telling Linda that I did not want to wake up one day at 50 years of age and wonder what if our Lord wanted us to have more children. So we did our research. We found that although it only had a 20% success rate for pregnancy, the sooner you did a re-tubaligation after the initial tube tying surgery, the greater your odds were at success. We had a better chance if we moved quickly. We learned that one of the risks of re-tubaligation surgery were tubal pregnancies due to scar tissue. A tubal pregnancy is where a fertilized egg is blocked and it implants itself on the scar tissue inside the fallopian tube rather than traveling to the woman's uterus to grow. It never makes it to the uterus. As the fertilized egg grows into an embryo, it eventually ruptures and the women can unknowingly bleed to death believing it is just her menstrual period. In 1992, Linda experienced this firsthand and if not for a planned shopping trip with our neighbor Linda Cross who lived next door, she would have bled to death. She had passed out on the floor and our neighbor Linda Cross came over after repeated telephone calls went unanswered. They were to go on a shopping trip together that afternoon. She found her and transported her to the hospital to find out what the problem was. They did corrective emergency surgery.

We had weighed this risk but decided to select a well-known doctor in Grand Rapids to perform the procedure Dr. Timothy Van Wingen. The surgery was performed at Butterworth Hospital three days before Christmas in 1988 which was the same hospital that Michael, Steven and Amber had all been born. That year it was our Christmas present to each other to have this surgery performed. Linda spent Christmas day in the hospital. It was one of the best presents we ever gave to each other!

On April 18, 1990, our fourth miracle entered the world when Mollie Lynn Williams was born at St. Mary's Hospital in Livonia, Michigan. She was an even 8 pounds and 20 inches long. The surgery had worked and we were once again on top of the world! It was difficult not to think of Michael. For each day of the first nine months of Mollie's life, she wore an electronic heart and breathing monitor when she slept. Whenever it went off, a loud audible alarm would sound, and it did so frequently. Each time the alarm would go off, we would race frantically into her bedroom with our hearts once again in our throats thinking "IT" was happening again, the SIDS. Every one of these episodes were false alarms where the wires had lost their contacts due to her rolling over or moving around in her crib.

On one occasion when Mollie was about three months old, she actually did stop breathing from a virus called RSV that she had contracted. Linda and I had taken CPR and she started CPR on Mollie that day while her parents who were in town visiting called 911. This happened right about 4:00 p.m. in the afternoon. I came home early that day from work, not knowing what was wrong. Linda's parents had come over from Grand Rapids to visit us, so Linda had instructed me to be home early that day if possible.

When I pulled up to our home there were three fire trucks and an EMS with lights and sirens blazing. As I stormed into the house, I saw my wife hysterical, my mother-in-law sobbing uncontrollably, my son Steven and daughter Amber wide-eyed and scared to death, and my father-in-law bawling. Mollie was on the counter with three or four firemen attending to her. I remember thinking at the time, "Oh no, here we go again!" That was the last thing I remember until two firemen were poking at me and shining a flashlight in my eyes. In the sudden catastrophe, I had fainted flat on my face and dropped like a bag of rocks on our kitchen floor. I dropped hard, too. Now they had two people to attend to. Thankfully, after Mollie spent the next week in the hospital, we learned that it had just been the RSV virus which had blocked her airway. It was still difficult to sleep at night. Each time the alarm sounded, it was as if the world was ending all over again. But we Buckled Our Chin Straps and got through this play, too!

Mollie grew stronger each day and soon before we knew it, she had made it through the danger zone and celebrated her first birthday. Once she was a year old we could return the heart and breathing monitor to the hospital. I was very happy to finally get rid of that contraption.

We were very thankful that the Lord gave us another child, another soul to help in His plans. I grew very close to Mollie and still am to this day. I think that after you have a child die, you really appreciate each child even more. The ones who are still alive you enjoy their journeys. You take nothing for granted anymore because you know as quickly as they are here, they can be gone. As they grow through childhood, adolescence, become teenagers and young adults, you view each passing day with them as a treasured gift. Believe me, your children should be your prized and most precious jewels because they really are!

I learned a very valuable lesson when Michael died. He taught me that you should NEVER take anyone you love and especially your child for granted. Cherish each minute, each hour and each day you get to spend with them. You never know when it may be your last.

Mollie was the light of our home to her sister Amber, brother Steven, Linda and me. As she grew up, my older children adored her and protected her. I never remember even one fight or sibling rivalry between her or for that matter any of my children. My children had already learned that life can be suddenly taken from you and squabbling and fighting over something trivial was not an acceptable behavior. I never had to tell them that or teach them that. They knew it instinctively because of what had happened to their little brother Michael. They knew already that our days here on earth are numbered so why quarrel.

Mollie lived a normal little girl's life. She grew up with birthday parties, dance lessons, sleepovers, pizza parties, vacations every year, and soccer. She loved as a little girl to play with her dolls and pretend she was a mama. At the time neither Linda nor I knew what was to become of her motherly instinct, but I think it was a foreshadowing of part of Michael's secret which Audrey had told me about.

Mollie was part of Michael's secret and as we later learned, so was Brayden. Maybe that is why Michael was smiling when he died. Through this experience, I have always thought that my dear Lord must have had a very important purpose or plan for Mollie. When you really stop and think about it, it took Michael's death to bring Mollie here. If Michael had lived, there is no way Mollie would ever have been born due to Linda's tubes being tied. Was Mollie getting pregnant as a teenager part of Michael's secret? Is this book and perhaps even the Michael's Wings Foundation to support poor teenage girls part of the secret? I do not know. What I do know is that God has His plan and I am willing to keep "Buckling My Chin Strap" to endure whatever His plans are and may be. If I am lucky, maybe I can find out what this secret of Michael's really is, before I, too, go home.

It is difficult to comprehend why things happen the way they do in life. All you can do is trust when things happen that it is part of God's plan and then go with it. Something good can come out of every bad situation, but you have to first accept it in faith. Once you accept it, then you have to look forward. The Lord put your eyes in the front of your head for a reason. He wants His servants to know that He wants them always focused on where they are going, not where they have been. When your teenage daughter gets pregnant, or your child dies, or you contract a rare disease, or some other type of disaster happens in your life, you must accept it in faith and look forward. "Buckle Your Chin Strap and Play the next Play."

It was through the Lord's gift of grace and faith that I was able to accept Michael's death at three months of age. The Lord had a plan. I did not know what His plan was. I simply had to accept it. I cannot blame Him for Michael's death as it was part of His plan. His plans are never wrong. I simply pray for the grace to accept it and move forward. Once I did accept it and move forward in faith, with Linda's re-tubaligation surgery, He rewarded us and blessed us with Mollie.

Now our precious Mollie has a son Brayden Michael Williams, our first grandchild. Mollie wanted to name Brayden's middle name "Michael" as a tribute to her brother whom she never even met. She knows that she is part of his secret and although she has never met him, she knows him. It was another difficult challenge both my wife and I along with Mollie had to overcome when she became pregnant at 16.

Please do not misunderstand what I am trying to convey here. I am not trying to encourage teenage pregnancy nor premarital sex. In fact, I hope as a father and mother you would use this story to inform your sons and daughters about the consequences of engaging in premarital sex and discuss that openly. I hope that your children will use abstinence and save themselves for the soulmate that God has planned for them to live their lives with.

Nevertheless, this teenage pregnancy did happen to Mollie and to our family. It was a test of our faith and our beliefs. We had to stand up for life and meet this problem head on. We had to look forward and do the right thing. I don't know how this will all fit into God's plan and Michael's secret, but I know with every fiber of my soul that God will make good out of what Satan intended as evil. Brayden Michael Williams was also part of God's plan and He wanted him to be here on this earth. Maybe Brayden or his offspring will do something extraordinary for the Lord or maybe he will just do the ordinary. Either way, Mollie and our family did God's will. Mollie gave him the precious gift of life and for that she can forever hold her head high. As a father you have to help your daughter through this trial of teenage pregnancy because it is definitely a test.

Now that you know the beginning of the story, I hope you can see why I placed it at the end. The "ends" in life, can always start a new beginning if you have faith. If you have trust in the Lord, the end only starts a new chapter. For me and my family, Michael's death was not the end of his life. It was the beginning. We still talk about him openly each and every day. He has not died. He is alive and part of his secret is alive in

Mollie and our new grandson, Brayden Michael Williams, her son. Someday I know I will hear the rest of his secret.

To demonstrate that Michael is still alive and can help poor teenage pregnant girls and their families, God will allow this book to be published. It is intended to help you as a father, a mother or maybe even a pregnant teen to have faith while in the storm. I have promised God that I will donate every single penny that this book makes to the foundation I will create named for my son, "Michael's Wings." The foundation will be set up to help the poor teenage girls who are pregnant and their families choose life. By choosing life and not death, God will show other families that only He can bring good out of what was intended for evil. Only He can help the teenage girls turn their lives around. Through the three pillars of education, faith and support, the foundation will help poor teenage girls have a life and a future. Their future will be one that includes promise and hope. It will only be through God's grace that "Michael's Wings" can spread His wings like Michael the Archangel of mercy and love to defend the defenseless and help bring life to the unborn.

*Jeremiah Chapter 1 Verse 5*
*"Before I formed you in the womb, I knew you; before you were born I dedicated you."*

Isn't it remarkable that before God even formed us in our mother's womb, He already knew us? This verse gives us wonderful guidance and direction as to what a teenage girl should do if she becomes pregnant. If God already knew the soul He formed, then you should leave it up to God to decide whether or not the child is born. You should choose to be responsible and accept the consequences of your error in judgment to engage in unprotected premarital sex. If you choose abortion, you are not only murdering another human being, but you are eliminating life for God's soul of the person He put in your womb.

Before each of us was born, God already had a plan for our lives and He dedicated us. What the plan is or will be is in many cases up to us to choose with our free will that He gave to us. The important thing is to try and do His will no matter how tough it may be.

When our daughter Mollie, the youngest of our four children, became pregnant at 16, it was a difficult challenge to face and overcome. Through God's grace, I was able to lead Mollie and my entire family through this storm. It is my sincere hope that this story fills you with hope. If your daughter is pregnant or should become pregnant as a teenager, as a man and as a father, you will need to Buckle Your Chin Strap.

My high school football coach Jim Crowley used to explain that you have never really been hit hard or hit anyone hard until your chin strap comes unbuckled. He would go on to say that when it does come unbuckled, you need to tighten it up one more notch, re-buckle it and play the next play. It was a very valuable lesson he taught to me. Little did I know at the time that his lesson would apply to my life experiences as a husband and as a father. Each time in my life that I have been hit so hard that my chin strap comes unbuckled, I notched it up another notch and I played the next play. My prayer is that as a father or mother you will do the same when the bad things come your way. Hopefully teenage pregnancy is not one of them. But rest assured, the bad things will come, and when they do, just "Buckle Your Chin Strap and play the next play!"

The one thing I would add to Coach Crowley's advice though, is that the only way you can re-buckle the chin strap sometimes and keep it snapped is by having a personal relationship with the Lord. Don't be afraid to start praying to Him each and every day. Attend church regularly and read His word in the Holy Bible. If you do these things I can guarantee you that when the hard-hit comes, you will be able to play the next play. The Lord will help you through it all just like He did me, my wife, my daughter and my family.

# Gratitude

There are so many people to thank who helped me in the writing of this book. The first person whom I would like to thank is my bride Linda. She endured many weekends where I would literally lock myself in the den to read and write. She also has persevered together with me through the journey of teenage pregnancy and losing our son Michael along with the raising of our three beautiful and living children Amber, Steven, and Mollie. She deserves a book to be written and dedicated to her. Her love has been the one constant I have had in my life that really blesses me. She is my best friend and soulmate. Maybe the next book can be dedicated to her!

I would like to thank Sylvia Pettigrew my secretary from work who typed the book at home in her spare time between raising her son and working. She took my handwritten notes and assembled them into the typed book format. She, too, has been a blessing in my life.

The cover of the book was designed by one of my oldest daughter's best friends who is a graphic artist. Her name is Danni Schertzing. She was absolutely phenomenal. Not only is she talented in her profession, but more importantly she has been a great friend to my oldest daughter Amber.

I would like to thank my cousin Debbie Richardson who told me the rest of her story that occurred when she became pregnant as a teenager. Her advice was one of many I received, and without a doubt was the one I appreciated the most. I just learned she became engaged this year at 54 years old, her first marriage. It seems the Lord is now blessing her life as she has found her son, and now her soulmate. I am truly happy for her.

I would like to thank my Men's Faith Sharing Group who helped and inspired me when I was going through this difficult time in my life. They were always there to comfort and challenge me.

I would like to thank my daughter Amber and son Steven for buckling their chin straps, too, and being there for their younger sister Mollie during this time. They, too, have experienced this whole journey and they were not only a tremendous blessing to me, I am quite sure they were for Mollie, too. In addition, each of them had their closest friends there to help them, Mollie and our family. Thanks to Megan, Travis, Katie, Mark, Jared and so many others too numerous to list who helped us.

My dad and his wife Rose were already great before they became GREAT grandpa and GREAT grandma. They were there to listen and counsel me all the way through this journey which was a tremendous blessing. Thanks to you both.

I would like to thank my brothers Dave and Joe whom I shared a bedroom with and also our college football dreams of playing together. I consider it an honor to have played on the same team with you two. I would also like to thank my sisters first Lizzie Belle who is always there whenever you need her and was there for Mollie; Lorie who has shown me how to battle through adversity by turning her life around, and Judy our baby sister who reminds me so much of my mother; "When the going gets tough the tough get going," right Judy or should I say Janny?

I would like to give a special thanks to Kristen Pertler for being Brayden's caregiver and much more to Mollie during Mollie's junior and senior years of high school. Kristen, I hope you know that you were a Godsend to our family! You are awesome!

Without Mollie's closest three friends she may have been lost. Morgan, Natalie and Samantha you guys were the best friends a teenage pregnant girl could ever have asked for. I saw the love you gave Mollie and will never forget it!

I would like to thank all the teachers who helped Mollie up at the Plymouth Canton Educational Park while she was pregnant, especially Mrs. Michelle Brunch, Mrs. Nicole McLeod, Mrs. Kristin Quesada, Mr. Bob Richardson, Mr. Jim Wheaton, Mrs. Kim Scully, Mrs. Mary Bard, Mrs. Mary Reading, Mrs. Nancy Gallagher, and the retired Superintendent Jim Ryan. You guys were fantastic to help Mollie get through High School, graduating on time.

Special thanks go out to Erin Wrenrick who was Mollie's fifth grade teacher who sent countless cards, notes and inspirational messages to Mollie and our family through the pregnancy journey. You are one of God's special angels. Keep your wonderful smile!

Many of my wife's Jazzercise and High School friends also were there for her and our family especially Jaye and John Chandler, Jaleena and Kevin Harrington, Linda and Jim Coburn, Andrea and Dan Kanaan, Kelly Perez, Patty Arizola, Patty Whymer, Jan Arizola, Janet Veen and many others. Thank you for helping Linda and me.

Our two friends, Bob and Linda Cross, have literally put out many fires in our life and were there for us once again even though our homes were no longer right next door. You two are a special couple!

I would like to thank all of my coaches who I had from high school to college on the gridiron who taught me the lessons I learned that have helped me live my life. I would especially like to thank Jim Crowley my high school head coach who is listening in heaven right now, Herb Brogan my high school position coach and friend, Jim Harkema my head college football coach who gave a skinny kid with six shirts a chance and a scholarship, and my dear friend and college position coach Bruce Zylstra. No Z, this was not, "Just like Saturday Night!"

I would like to thank my special friends at work and in the community who encouraged me to write this book and keep it going from Jeff Coon, Tom Menard, Ed Saplala, Marijana Zlateska, Nelson Brikho, Dave Morgan, Randy Roys, Charlene Borke, the Tonda Elementary staff, and my choir mates from both St. John Neumann and Resurrection Catholic Churches, singing was a way to strengthen and recommit my resolve.

Special thanks to Mike McGee a personal friend, who helped counsel me on setting up the "Michael's Wings" Foundation and brought me together with Schoolcraft College for the joining of the Foundation to their college for scholarships and daycare for the Detroit Metropolitan teenage girls who need the help.

Many others helped contribute to this book in my every day living and writing as well. Some of my customers even got into the act and some of them including Deb Coffing, Scott Keith and Tom Wilson shared their perspectives from the other parent side of the journey as each of them had sons who had the same thing happen to them. Other customers like Bob

Beckley, Bill Bohlen and Suzanne Moreno simply encouraged me to write it and finish it. Even my dentist and friend Frank Kelly gave me six month pep talks from a father who had been there in a similar experience.

I would like to thank my special editor Mary Beckley who as an English major, was able to provide perfect editing all the way from Surprize, Arizona! Thank you Mary, Bob sure was lucky to find you!

Finally, I would like to thank two people whom I have never met, but helped me publish this book. The first is Theresa Tomeo whom I listen regularly to on 990am Catholic radio. Second, I would like to thank Cheryl Dickow, my publisher, who gave me the chance to publish the book with her. She gave advice and was extremely patient with a rookie who was just trying to do what God told him to do.

For all these people I mentioned and those who I could not or forgot, please accept my heartfelt appreciation for being an inspiration and part of my life. I am truly blessed for having the blessing of each of you to share our time here together. May God Bless and keep you all forever in His grace.

# THE DEDICATION OF THE BOOK

When I started to write this book I wondered if I would ever finish it. My goal was to be complete with it by December 31, 2008. Right now it is December 30th, 2008 and I am nearly finished one whole day ahead of schedule! As I thought of who to dedicate this book to, it was a no-brainer. I knew immediately who they would be.

Basically, it comes down to three people the first and most important are my parents. They are most important because without them I would not be here writing this book today. Without my parents I would never have learned the values for which I stand. They taught me to live being honest and to always stand with integrity in anything you do. They sacrificed for all six of us kids so that we could attend catholic schools for all twelve years of our elementary and high school education. My mother, God rest her soul, Janet Fern Williams, always told me that she was going to write a book. She had a very challenging life in which she had to pick up and move to a new house and city over a hundred times in her childhood being raised by two alcoholic nomadic parents who moved around the country to avoid the bill collectors. She never got to write her story after she retired early to write it, she died two months later at age 60. Mom, this book is a tribute to you and what you did not get to write. I hope it makes you proud in heaven.

Dad, you were the epitome of the father I needed and wanted to become someday when it was my turn to be a dad. I will never forget how you worked in the "Iron Jungle" for me, my brothers and sisters and all the other odd jobs you did just so we could have the things we had. Thank you! More importantly, you taught me to trust in my instincts and to believe in myself. With the challenges I have faced in my life, I don't know if I would have made it had I not had a good example of what to be and how to do the tough things. Thanks, Dad I love you!

The next person that I would like to dedicate this book to is Brayden Michael Williams, my grandson. Brayden, someday you will grow up into a man and a father. You will always have this book to share with your children what the journey was really like for your mother when she was a scared and frightened 16 year old girl in a large suburban high school. It took a lot of courage, strength and guts for her to take responsibility for her actions and live with the consequences. You are the consequence and a most blessed one at that. She will undoubtedly sacrifice a lot for you, so love her and be an obedient son. Someday you will have the pressures to engage in premarital sex with girls in high school and college. When those temptations come, run and say NO! Ask the Lord to help you deny these temptations.

God has a special plan for your life. You would not be here without your mother's courage to do the right thing and give up many of her dreams. You need to love your mom, help her always and remember that you will always be God's beloved son. Your Uncle Michael died at 3 months of age and had a secret. You are part of that secret and you need to live out that legacy with your life being a faithful servant of God and passing it on to your children and their children! I want to see you in heaven and all of them, too.

I hope I live long enough to see you one day marry your bride and the soulmate that the Lord has ordained for you. If not, love her, be faithful to her and remember that marriage is a covenant with her and

God. Covenants with God cannot be broken until death so stay faithful to your bride and do not be tempted by divorce like the throw away society we live in encourages. Remember to study hard since education is the key to the future for you and your family. Work hard and do not be afraid to sweat and get blisters on your hands. They are character builders. Remember that God has forgiven you of your sins through the precious blood of His Son Jesus Christ so forgive others who hurt you in life. Take time to enjoy the simple things in life. Learn from trials. Don't be afraid to sing and make music with an instrument; it is God's gift to the soul. Tell your kids about your "Grand PA" Williams and teach them the lessons in this book. Finally, always remember that I love you and I am very happy that God put you in our family!

Finally, the last person who I want to dedicate this book to is my precious daughter Mollie. You are quite a courageous and tough young lady Mollie! I must admit that I was shocked when we found out that you were pregnant. You surprised us not only with the news, but how you handled everything. I told you when Brayden was born that you are now one of my heroes! I really meant that! To endure what you did and make the tough decisions that you did, showed a resolve in your character beyond your years. You stood for life and took responsibility for your actions. The fact that you finished high school on time while being abandoned by Brayden's father says a lot about the depth of your soul. Many other girls would have dropped out. I was so proud of you! You made tough decisions from a Godly Christian perspective after you made a poor decision to engage in premarital sex. I know you know that your life will not be easy. There will be times that it will be tough, but I really think that when you reflect back on what you already have endured, you will be able to get through it. This book is entitled "Buckle Your Chin Strap" because I told it from a father's perspective in what I went through as I tried to help you, mom and the rest of our family battle through this challenge. You proved to me that you are worthy of the title. Every step of your journey you buckled up the chin strap. Whether it was coming to grips with being 16 and pregnant, carrying Brayden in your body, morning sickness, your boyfriend abandoning you, holding down a job, studying and getting much better grades, labor, delivery of Brayden, late night feedings when having school or work the next day, and all the demands on your time of being a mom. To your credit I have NEVER ONCE heard you complain. That is phenomenal. I truly admire you for that, Mollie.

My prayer for you going forward is that you remember to keep buckling your chin strap when you are raising Brayden and going through your life. There will be many times you will be exhausted, disappointed and stressed over everyday life and the raising of Brayden. Remember to BUCKLE THAT CHIN STRAP and ask the Lord to help you. You, too, are part of your brother Michael's secret. I think that you are one of the biggest reasons he smiled when he died. He probably saw you and "Cheeks" and your offspring and the marvelous things you all are going to do in this world to witness for God. No matter what happens to you in life remember that you can do anything with the Lord by your side. One day, I will have to leave and go to heaven. I will be there waiting for you. Make sure that you are there too, and all my grandkids. Do your job with them and make sure they know who the Lord Jesus is and what gift He has freely given to them. Love you TONS DADDIO!